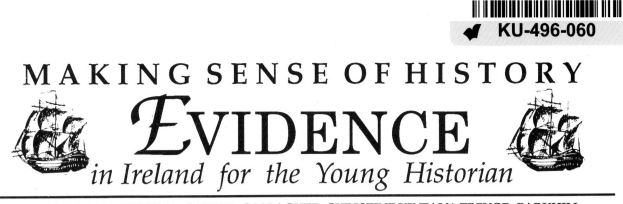

MAKING SENSE OF HISTORY
EVIDENCE
in Ireland for the Young Historian

GENERAL EDITORS   CARMEL GALLAGHER CHRISTINE KINEALY TREVOR PARKHILL

The Editors
CARMEL GALLAGHER, CHRISTINE KINEALY, TREVOR PARKHILL
wish to acknowledge
warmly the contributions of
NICK BRANNON, DEIRDRE BROWN, CATHAL DALLAT,
ANNE FAY, ANN HAMLIN, BRIAN LAMBKIN,
ROBERT MCKINLEY AND MARION MEEK.
The Editors alone, however, are responsible for the text.

ULSTER HISTORICAL FOUNDATION
PUBLICATIONS

Published 1990
by the Ulster Historical Foundation
68 Balmoral Avenue
Belfast
Northern Ireland

This book has received financial assistance under the Cultural Traditions Programme,
which aims to encourage acceptance and understanding of cultural diversity.

ISBN 0 901 905 43 7

Printed by Graham & Sons (Printers) Ltd.
51 Gortin Road
Omagh
Co. Tyrone

Cover designed by Wendy Dunbar

CONTENTS

ACKNOWLEDGMENTS

The Editors would like, on behalf of the Trustees of the Ulster Historical Foundation, to thank the following people and institutions who have given their permission for the reproduction of extracts from, or photographs of, sources in their possession, for which they are responsible: Mr. Michael Duffin, for the extracts from Emma Duffin's diaries; the National Gallery of Ireland for the illustrations of Broighter Hoard and St. Patrick's Bell and Shrine; the Deputy Keeper of the Public Record Office of Northern Ireland for extracts from Ordnance Survey maps, school registers, the Harland and Wolff poster and Ahoghill cholera notice (PRONI O.S.6/5/7/1-4, SCH 1088, D.2910 and D.2084/1/3 respectively); the Ulster Folk and Transport Museum and the Archaeological Survey of Northern Ireland for photographs in their possession. Warm thanks are also due to Dr. Patrick Buckland, Dr. A. T. Q. Stewart and Professor David Harkness for, respectively, extracts from *Irish Unionism 1885-1923: a Documentary History* (1973), *The Ulster Crisis* (1966), and *The Idea of History* (BBC Radio 1989).

C. Gallagher
C. Kinealy
T. Parkhill

FOREWORD

It is now taken for granted in history teaching at all levels that systematic use should be made of the documentary and other evidence which historians examine in re-creating and analysing our past. Quite often, however, this is easier said than done. If they are to prove appropriate, source materials must relate not only to the topics and periods to be studied, but also to the ages and circumstances of the pupils concerned. In this latter connection there remains a dearth of Irish source materials, particularly those suitable for use by younger age groups. The primary purpose of *Making Sense of History* is to meet this need for the age group 12 to 16.

We hope that in using this book pupils will be introduced to a wide range of different types of evidence, both documentary and visual. They will also be encouraged to make judgements about the strengths and weaknesses, the reliability or the limitations, of this evidence. The intention is to demonstrate that items of evidence need to be weighed and are rarely of equal value; that they are sometimes in conflict, if not flatly contradictory; and that they are commonly the subject of differing interpretations by those who use them.

The objective is to awaken pupils to the richness, variety and complexity of historical evidence and to enable them to learn about the way in which historians go about their work. Simultaneously, they will emerge with a keener appreciation of the cultural heritage of the particular part of the world in which they live.

Peter Roebuck
Chairman, Publications Committee
Ulster Historical Foundation

TO THE PUPIL

How do we know about the past?

How are history books written?

How reliable is the evidence of the past?

This book will help you find out about the different types of EVIDENCE which historians study before they write about Irish history. It also contains examples of this evidence, on which you will be able to carry out your own research. Some sources are very rare and are the only remaining evidence of a time in the past. Other periods, especially the recent past, have lots of evidence which must be tested for bias and accuracy. This book provides background information about each type of evidence, and advice on how it might be used. The aim is to help you to develop the skills of a young historian.

TO THE TEACHER

The recent emphasis in history teaching has been on the study of evidence in the classroom. This book provides teachers with detailed information on the range and nature of sources available for the study of Irish history. An explanation of each source is accompanied by practical examples and questions which have been chosen with the secondary school pupil aged 12-16 in mind. The sources are arranged in sections:

ARCHAEOLOGICAL
ARTEFACTS
WRITTEN
PRINTED
PHOTOGRAPHIC
ORAL

These are presented chronologically and each section contains its own questions.

The aim is to give the pupil an informed outline of the different forms of evidence which historians of Irish history, from pre-Christian times to the present day, must research. It will also provide the teacher with the basis for a number of patch studies of important periods in Irish history, using the evidence in its several forms.

ARCHAEOLOGY AND ARCHAEOLOGISTS

What is Archaeology?

Archaeology is the study of the past by examining the physical remains that people have left behind them. These remains may be sites, monuments or artefacts. Sites or monuments are places where people lived, worshipped or were buried. Artefacts may be broken pieces of pottery, weapons, bones or personal possessions.

When archaeologists are excavating a site they carefully dig down and sift through each layer of soil, searching for any artefacts which may be buried in it. These layers have built up, one on top of another, over the centuries. Generally speaking, the deeper down archaeologists dig, the further back in time they go and the older are the artefacts which they uncover. The artefacts within each layer of soil give clues as to what life was like when the layer was created.

Just as fragments of ancient pottery are pieced together in an attempt to show what the original container was like, in the same way fragments of information preserved in the ground can reveal a lot about the past. An archaeologist can work out the size and shape of a timber building just from the pattern of holes left by wooden posts driven into the ground, even though the posts have rotted away. The smallest pieces of the past, such as fish bones or pollen grains, can provide valuable evidence about the food people ate and the type of agriculture they used. Unless the digging is done carefully, these tiny but vital pieces can be missed.

Excavation of an early Christian period house at Deer Park Farms, County Antrim.

Excavations

Archaeologists realise that while excavation reveals a great deal of information, it can also be destructive. They therefore only excavate when they know a site is going to be destroyed or built upon. Archaeologists spend only some of their time on 'digs'. Much of their time is spent visiting and surveying sites. They then look for any other details they can find from records such as old maps or photographs. This is all put together into a sort of archaeological encyclopaedia called a *Sites and Monuments Record* (or SMR).

Archaeological sites are an important part of any country's heritage so archaeologists try to protect and preserve them. In Northern Ireland 13,000 archaeological sites and monuments have been identified. Some sites are protected by law, although most of them are in private ownership. Archaeologists encourage owners to respect and value them. They advise on careful and sympathetic conservation of these sites so that the public can visit and enjoy their heritage.

QUESTIONS

1. What kinds of artefacts may be found on ancient sites?
2a. Why is excavation destructive?
  b. Can you think of the many different ways destruction might be caused to an archaeological site?
3. Archaeologists are often asked 'Have you found any treasure?', as though this is the point of their excavations. But compare the coins in your pocket or your purse with the contents of your dustbin at home. Which do you think tells you more about you and your family and the way you live, and why?
4. Compare your home with your school or a church that you know. If you could revisit their ruins in 500 years, what parts of them do you think would have survived? What parts of the buildings would give you clues as to how they were used? List the sort of 'finds' that you might discover and those which would have decayed and vanished.

GLOSSARY

artefact — an object made or shaped by man
excavation — to expose by digging, sometimes by hand
conservation — the means of preserving from decay

ARCHAEOLOGICAL SITES:
1. RATHS AND SOUTERRAINS

The most common archaeological features in the Ulster landscape today are raths and earthworks dating from the Early Christian period. Raths are also known as forts, ringforts or forths. The Early Christian period spans the years between around AD 450 to about AD 1200. As many as 30,000-40,000 raths were built in Ireland during this period. Not all of them have survived centuries of destruction.

Raths

The remains of a typical rath look like a circular space about 35 metres across, surrounded by a low bank, perhaps 3-4 metres wide and 2 metres high. The outer ditch may be visible as a shallow hollow with a causeway across it. Raths were mostly built in good lowland farming areas, usually on a slight slope to help drainage and facing south to get the sunshine. They were generally used for farmsteads and would have included timber buildings, sometimes with stone foundations. In some areas raths made entirely of stone have been found. These are known as cashels. Crops were grown and animals were kept in the fields around the buildings. Some of the raths had a defensive purpose against predatory animals like wolves, hit-and-run cattle raiders or slave-traders. Over 50 examples of raths in Northern Ireland have been excavated. A rath which was excavated at Ballywee, near Parkgate in County Antrim, revealed well-preserved traces of houses with stone hearths, outbuildings, stone paths and drains.

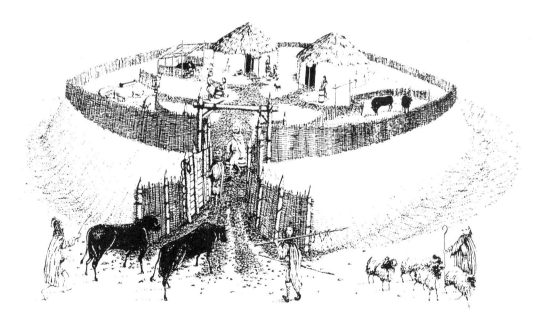

Reconstruction drawing of Early Christian period rath.

What would you find in a rath?

Animal bones are often found when raths are excavated. These bones are clues to what people ate. The bones may also indicate what animals were being bred on the site and at what ages they were killed. Other finds have included crude hand-made pottery known as 'souterrain ware', stone querns for grinding grain, whetstones for sharpening tools, and glass beads, presumably for necklaces or bracelets.

Certain weather conditions help to preserve archaeological remains better than others. Recent excavations of waterlogged layers in a rath at Deer Park Farms, County Antrim, have revealed a wealth of organic remains which, under normal dry circumstances, would have decayed and vanished long ago. Here the remains of circular houses were found. The archaeologists were able to work out that the walls had been constructed from woven wattles and the cavity between them stuffed with vegetation.

When the midden material was examined, it was found to be rich with environmental evidence such as insect remains, seeds, and the eggs of parasitic worms. It also contained wooden bucket staves, leather shoes, and a wooden shoe-last on which some of the shoes had been made.

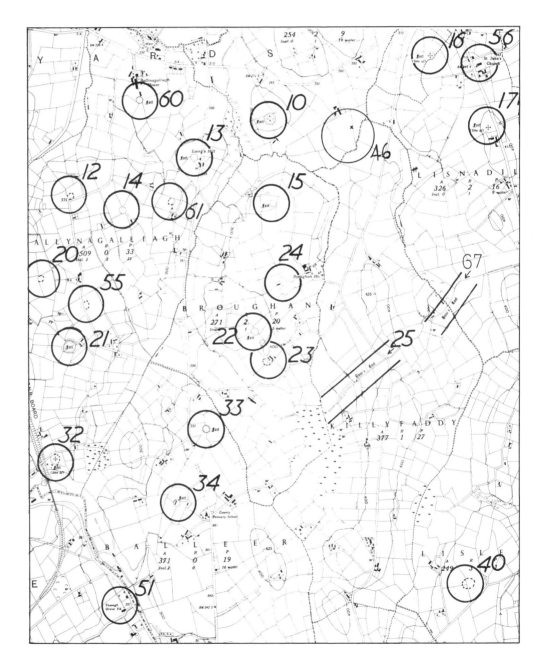

Raths shown on a County Armagh Ordnance Survey map.

Many raths had souterrains below them. These were concealed man-made caves or underground tunnels which archaeologists think would have been used as hidey-holes for people and their valuables when their raths were attacked. Some souterrains were tunnelled from rock, but usually they were made by digging a trench into the earth and walling and roofing it with large stones. It was then covered over with soil to make it invisible from the ground above. Some souterrains are simple tunnels. Others are more complex with interconnecting chambers separated by narrow 'creeps'. They may also have such features as air vents, blind alleys or be built on a split level.

While souterrains may be fascinating to explore, they can be cramped, wet and dangerous. You should not venture into one without adequate clothing and lights, or without informing somebody above ground of your whereabouts.

Many archaeological sites have stories or superstitions associated with them, often about fairies or curses. Souterrains are no exception. In the early 19th century some men tried to open a souterrain in Hillis' Fort, in Tullintanvally townland, parish of Annaclone, County Down. After they started work "horses were heard rushing . . . from all sides". The excavation attempt was abandoned and has never been started again.

QUESTIONS

1. See how many 'forts' you can identify in this County Armagh map.
2. Why were stone forts, or cashels, built?
3. Archaeologists rarely find human remains in raths. What do you think happened to the people who lived and died there?
4. What could souterrains be used for?
5. Where did souterrain builders obtain their stones?

GLOSSARY

wattle — flexible sticks woven to make walls or roofs
midden material — household rubbish

ARCHAEOLOGICAL SITES:
2. THE GIANT'S RING

Archaeologist surveying the Giant's Ring.

What is the Giant's Ring?

The Giant's Ring is a good example of an archaeological site. It is simply an unusual pile of stones surrounded by an earthen bank. The stone arrangement was not created by nature so we can assume it was built by people who lived a long time ago. Because it is so old, there are no written records to explain the purpose of the Giant's Ring. It is therefore necessary for archaeologists to try to understand the reasons why it was constructed and the uses to which it was put.

In 1954 an archaeologist, Mr Pat Collins, dug a narrow slice out of the bank of earth which surrounds the stones. He was able to work out how the bank had been made but he also said:

> *The date and function of the Giant's Ring are still mysterious and (my) excavations have done little to clear away the mystery.*

Because Mr Collins was the last person to excavate the site, much of the mystery remains. Many questions are still unanswered such as:

Who built the Giant's Ring?

Why was this location chosen?

How did they move the stones into position?

Why were the stones arranged in this way?

An entry in a guide book called *Historic Monuments of Northern Ireland*, which was written after Mr Collins' excavation, says:

> *The date and function of the monument are both difficult to establish. It maybe was a late Neolithic ceremonial or assembly site.*

'Neolithic' is the New Stone Age period which lasted from 4000 BC- 2500 BC.

No evidence has ever been found of people living inside the Ring. This might suggest that the Giant's Ring was used only for meetings or gatherings. Some archaeologists, however, have suggested that the stones inside may be the remains of a 'Passage Grave' (an ancient burial site), similar to the one at Newgrange, County Meath.

Archaeologists, like historians, base their information on the evidence which they find. The Giant's Ring is a good example of a story which remains unexplained because the evidence is insufficient. Archaeologists therefore must make educated guesses about this site. This is made easier if they are able to make comparisons with other similar sites.

Apart from Newgrange, the Giant's Ring can also be compared to other similar structures elsewhere. The most famous of these is Stonehenge in Wiltshire, England — 'henge' means a large, circular, embanked structure.

EXERCISES

Say whether you agree or disagree with the following statements:
(a) It is impossible to know anything about the past unless you have evidence.
(b) Archaeologists can find out all about what happened in the past before the invention of writing.
(c) The Giant's Ring is a complete mystery.
(d) A reasonable guess by a professional archaeologist is more valuable than a guess by an untrained amateur.
(e) It is usually impossible to find out everything we would like to know about what happened in the past.
(f) Archaeologists can find out about things which other historians cannot, and vice-versa.
(g) The findings of archaeologists about things made before the invention of writing can be very helpful to historians.

FIND OUT MORE ABOUT:

(1) ARCHAEOLOGICAL SITES LIKE THE GIANT'S RING
   The most important ones on the island of Ireland are described in
   (a) *Historic Monuments of Northern Ireland* (HMSO, 1987) (covering the 6 counties of Northern Ireland)
   (b) *Guide to the National Monuments of Ireland* (26 counties of Republic of Ireland)
(2) THE WORK OF ARCHAEOLOGISTS
   (a) *Pieces of the Past* (HMSO, 1988) (covering the 6 counties)
   (b) P. Harbinson, *Pre-Christian Ireland from the First Settlers to the Early Celts* (Thames and Hudson, 1988) (covering the 32 counties)

ARTEFACTS AS NON-WRITTEN EVIDENCE

When there is little written evidence available about early civilisations, historians must use a variety of other sources to find out how people lived. In addition to the archaeological sites, historians and archaeologists can also use artefacts and folklore as evidence.

The Broighter Hoard

One of the greatest collections of Iron Age artefacts is known as the Broighter Hoard. It dates from the first century BC. It includes a miniature gold boat complete with oars, and a magnificent decorated gold necklace or torc. These were discovered in 1854 by a farmer who was working in his field in the townland of Broighter near Limavady, County Londonderry. He was using a new plough and stopped to lift a stone in case it damaged the plough. He discovered a wooden box. When it was opened, it was found to contain the treasures which we now call the Broighter Hoard. The artistic detail on these items is similar to decorations found on Iron Age treasures in Switzerland. Examine the illustration below.

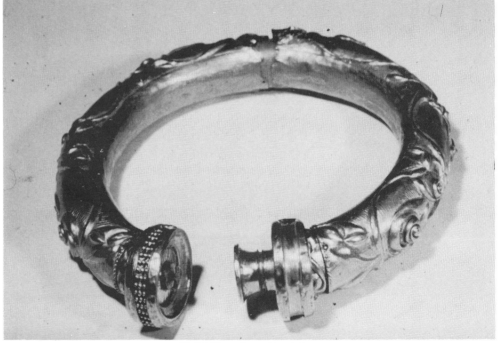

Gold Torc from Broighter.

St. Patrick's Bell and Shrine

St. Patrick's Bell itself is made of iron bent into shape and riveted together, then dipped in bronze. High crosses and other carved stones often show churchmen carrying bells like this.
(Adapted from *Treasures of Early Irish Art* (1977)).
The keeping of ancient relics, many of them from biblical times, played an important part in the role of the church in the Middle Ages. They were the links between the churches that were established at the time of Christ, and the newly built churches of the Middle Ages. Because of this, relics were very popular as well as valuable, and people were very keen to buy them. They were often bought and sold and, of course, fake relics were often substituted for the real thing.

One of the most valuable Irish relics is the Bell of St. Patrick and the Shrine which was made to protect it. Little is known of the early life of St. Patrick and, although we know a good deal about his later life as a missionary in Ireland, no-one knows where he was buried. The precise date of his death in the 5th century is not known. We do know, however, that in 553AD the *Annals of Ulster*, one of the earliest written records in Irish history, recorded that his tomb had been opened by St. Columba. St. Columba removed three items — a Book, a Goblet and a Bell. The Bell went missing for over 4 centuries. The Book and the Goblet have never been found.

When we next hear of the Bell, it is accompanied by a Shrine. Shrines were used to protect ancient relics. The Shrine for St. Patrick's Bell is helpful because it has an inscription on it, in Irish: *Or do Domhnall U Lachlaind lasin dernad in clocsa.* When translated it reads: *A prayer for Domhnall Ua Lochlainn who caused this Shrine to be made.*

We know that Domhnall Ua Lochlainn was high king of the northern Uí Néill clan around 1100 AD.

After the fourteenth century, St. Patrick's Bell and Shrine disappeared and no mention of them was made in the written records of this time.

Folklore, which had been handed down from generation to generation since the Middle Ages, claimed that these treasures had been entrusted to the care of two families, the Mulhollands and the Mellons.

In the nineteenth century, St. Patrick's Bell and Shrine were discovered in the possession of an old man named Mulholland who came from just north of the shores of Lough Neagh, an area which had been the ancestral home of the Mulholland clan. Mr. Mulholland, who had no remaining relatives, gave the treasure to his local doctor who had looked after him until he died.

St. Patrick's Bell and the Shrine which belongs to it can now be seen in the National Museum in Dublin.

Shrine of St. Patrick's Bell.

EXERCISE 1

THE BROIGHTER HOARD

1. Why do you think the Broighter Hoard got its name?
2. How can you tell that this part of Co. Londonderry was inhabited in the first century BC?
3. By looking at the gold torc, how skilled do you think the inhabitants were in metal working?
4. Can you be sure these objects were made in Ireland?
5. How can you tell that the people valued gold ornaments?
6. How could historians tell if the Hoard was genuine?

EXERCISE 2

ST. PATRICK'S BELL AND SHRINE

1. How do we know how old these artefacts are?
2. What evidence is there to suggest that these artefacts are associated with St. Patrick?
3. (a) Why were relics important to the early Church?
   (b) Why are relics important to historians?
   (c) What is their value as evidence?
4. What type of evidence is there to link St. Patrick's Bell and Shrine to the area north of Lough Neagh?

BUILDINGS

A building tells us as much about who built it and who used it as any written evidence does. Unfortunately, many decay or are destroyed, or they may be altered by gradual change so that their original features are hard to recognise. Nevertheless, the experienced observer can work on the evidence which survives to uncover lots of details about life in the past times. The older the building, the greater is its value as evidence.

Tower-Houses

The tower-houses of County Down illustrate how much can be learnt from buildings. Roughly 30 good examples survive. We know of several more which have not survived, or have only partly survived. Other parts of Ireland have far more tower-houses: for example, there are more than 400 tower-houses in Limerick and more than 300 in Cork. A tower-house is a small defensive structure in which the main element is a stone tower. Tower-houses were built from the early 15th century to the early 17th century by important people who needed to protect their wealth from attack. Each area has its own distinctive style, reflecting changes in social needs and styles of warfare over the 200 years.

An interior of Kilclief Castle, Co. Down.

Machicolation, Strangford Castle, County Down.

Window seats on Audley's Castle, Co. Down.

Fifteenth-century Tower-Houses: Kilclief Castle and Audley's Castle

Kilclief Castle, and Audley's Castle in Co. Down, were both built in the first half of the 15th century. Kilclief, which has an elegant tower 60m high, was the summer residence of John Sely, Bishop of Down. The quality of its window details suggests that the builders may have been church masons. Both towers had two projecting turrets with a high arch between them. One turret contained the entrance and a spiral staircase, the other a series of toilets (known as garderobes). The entrance door was impossible to charge because it was concealed on the inner face of the tower.

Why did the Bishop of Down need to live in a castle like Kilclief? A bishop was a landlord, with all the powers and duties of a nobleman. The Bishop of Down was a wealthy man, with valuables to protect. His income came mostly from the land. Rent was paid to him in the form of barley and beef and he sold some of it in exchange for imported wine and cloth. His needs were similar to those of his neighbour John Audley who lived in Audley's Castle.

Inside Kilclief and Audley's Castle there are many features which provide evidence of its date. The main cooking was probably done outdoors, or in a separate kitchen, but each tower had a room with fireplace, built-in cupboards, and a slop-hole (a garbage disposal chute) used for tidying up after the meal. The bigger windows, high up in the tower, facing into the courtyard, were fitted with window-seats, allowing enough light for reading or sewing.

Sixteenth-century Tower-Houses: Narrow Water Castle

Narrow Water is built on a strategic point where Carlingford Lough has narrowed to the Newry River, a point suitable for a ferry. The Normans built a small earth-work castle nearby guarding this important route. The tower-house was built in the 16th century entirely with government money, which means that we have more details of its construction than we would have from a privately built castle. The cost of construction was £361 4s 2d, paid in 1570. The Treasurer-at-war's account describes it as:

> One new castle within which are two chambers and a cellar and a hall covered with straw and a stable nigh unto the said castle . . . and nine cottages covered with earth within the precinct of the said castle.

All that is left today is the tower and its precinct wall, known in Ireland as the bawn. The cottages and stable were less well constructed and have not survived. Narrow Water is an excellent example of a defensive building. There were two entrances to the bawn, one on the South to the river, guarded by a small turret, and the other to the North. If the enemy broke in either of these, he would not be able to charge the tower door which was on the West side. The door was protected by a porch, again preventing a direct charge. The porch had no roof so if the enemy got in he could be bombarded from a drop hole (machicolation) directly above. Inside the door was a murder-hole.

Many tower-houses have an additional internal protection, of a stone vault, immediately below the lord's main chamber. This prevented the defenders from being burnt out of the tower and, as the stairs were also stone-built, they were also fire-proof.

Reconstructed drawing of Narrow Water Castle, Co. Down.

Later Tower-Houses

By the early 17th century new weapons were in use, and this is reflected in the way later tower-houses were built. Instead of long arrowslits, round musket-loops were fitted, as in Quoile Castle and Kirkistown Castle. There were so many gun-loops in Quoile Castle, defenders would have had to cover three or more holes each! Another feature of later tower-houses is extra rooms. By the 17th century, people no longer wished to share accommodation, and bed chambers were added.

QUESTIONS

1. The chief surviving tower-houses of County Down are at Narrow Water, Ardglass, Kilclief, Strangford, Portaferry, Sketrick, Ringhaddy, Audley's, Old Castle Ward, Walshestown, Quoile and Dromore. Find as many as you can on a map. What does their location suggest to us about defence and commerce?

2. The most vulnerable points of a castle are its doors and windows.
   (a) How did tower-houses attempt to protect these weak points?
   (b) Can you pick out differences between 15th, 16th, and 17th century defences?

MAPS

Maps are needed to let people know where natural features such as fields, mountains and rivers are located. They also show where buildings, roads and bridges have been built.

Maps became important in the sixteenth and seventeenth centuries. At this time, English and Scottish settlers were sold land in Ireland. They needed maps to show the boundaries of their new properties. Before a map could be made, the land had to be examined by a SURVEYOR. It was then drawn by a CARTOGRAPHER, who needed to be skilled in mathematics, geometry and drawing. Both the surveyors and the cartographers needed to be fit as they were required to measure carefully on foot huge areas of Ireland owned by the new proprietors.

In the early part of the seventeenth century the county of Coleraine was taken over by 12 London Companies who renamed it County Londonderry. The London Companies employed Sir Thomas Phillips in 1622 to carry out a survey of the lands they owned. He then employed a cartographer, called Thomas Raven, to draw maps of this property.

One of the main features of the settlement of Londonderry was the construction of a town, Coleraine, which stood on the River Bann close to the north coast.

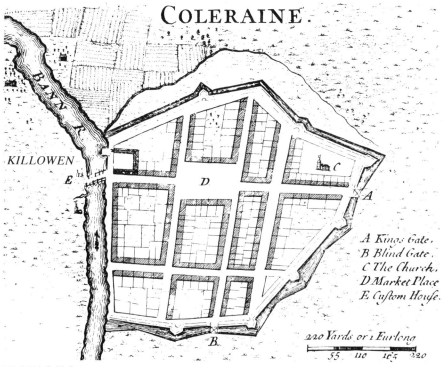

COLERAINE

A Kings Gate,
B Blind Gate,
C The Church,
D Market Place
E Custom House.

220 Yards or 1 Furlong
55   110   165   220

QUESTIONS

This is a map of the town of Coleraine in 1622.

1. The title refers to it as being 'fortified'. Examine the map closely and explain what is meant by a fortified town.
2. Do you think the houses across the river, in Killowen, are part of the fortified town? Who do you think lived in them?
3. How can you tell the town was built to a planned design?
4. Do you think the bridge (marked E) is new?
5. Look at the key to the map of the town. What evidence is there that it is planned to be a centre of trade and business?
6. What are the advantages of a fortified town being built on a river?

Ordnance Survey Maps

The first mapping of all of Ireland, on a standard scale of 6 inches to 1 mile, was undertaken in the 1830s. It was carried out by the Ordnance officers of the part of the British Army known as the Royal Engineers. It was therefore called the Ordnance Survey and continues to be known as that today.

Each part of Ireland was mapped in the 1830s, the 1860s, the 1900s and in the 1930s. It is, therefore, possible to find evidence of continuity and change if you compare the maps of one particular area from the 1830s to the 1930s. You will find on the following pages Ordnance Survey maps of Coleraine for 1833, 1859 and 1933. Answer the questions below by referring to these three Ordnance Survey maps of the town. You can study any area, in the town or countryside, in Northern Ireland by a similar comparison of the various editions of Ordnance Survey maps. You have already seen (on p.14) that Ordnance Survey maps record the presence of archaeological sites, such as raths and souterrains, in rural areas. They also show where churches, schools, forges, etc. were to be found. The maps of Coleraine will let you see how they can be used to study the growth of towns.

QUESTIONS

1. What evidence is there on the 1833 map of Coleraine of the walled town in 1622?
2. Compare the 1833 and 1859 maps:
   (a) What new form of transport is evident?
   (b) Has this anything to do with the new bridge, to the north of the town?
   (c) What was the workhouse? Was it unique to Coleraine?
3. Why do you think the fever hospital was so far from the town?
4. Study the 1933 map. What evidence of the pre-Plantation period has been mapped on this but not on earlier maps? Why do you think the earlier maps did not record these features?
5. Compare the growth of the town between 1622 and 1833, and then from 1833 to 1933. What do the maps tell you about the development of the town of Coleraine? When did it develop most?
6. Maps are mostly used by geographers. From your study of maps such as these, how can maps help historians?

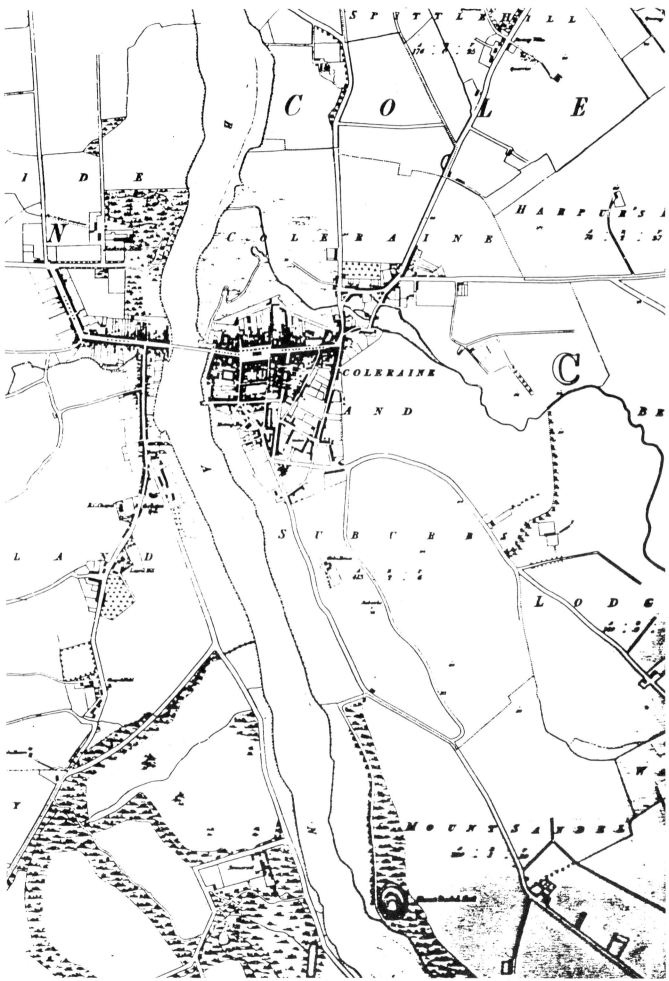

Ordnance Survey map of Coleraine, 1833.

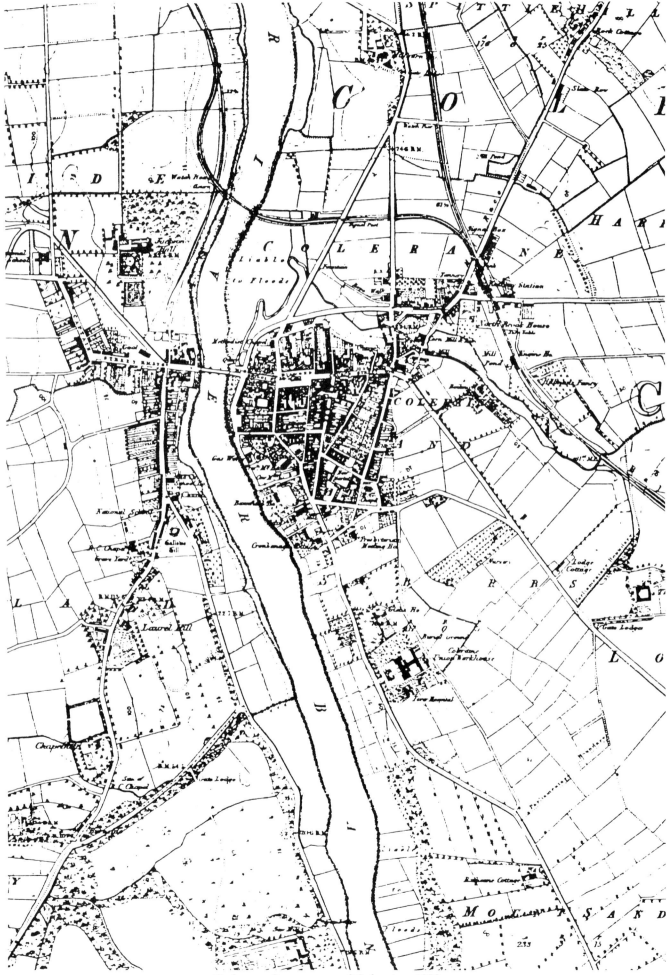

Ordnance Survey map of Coleraine, 1859.

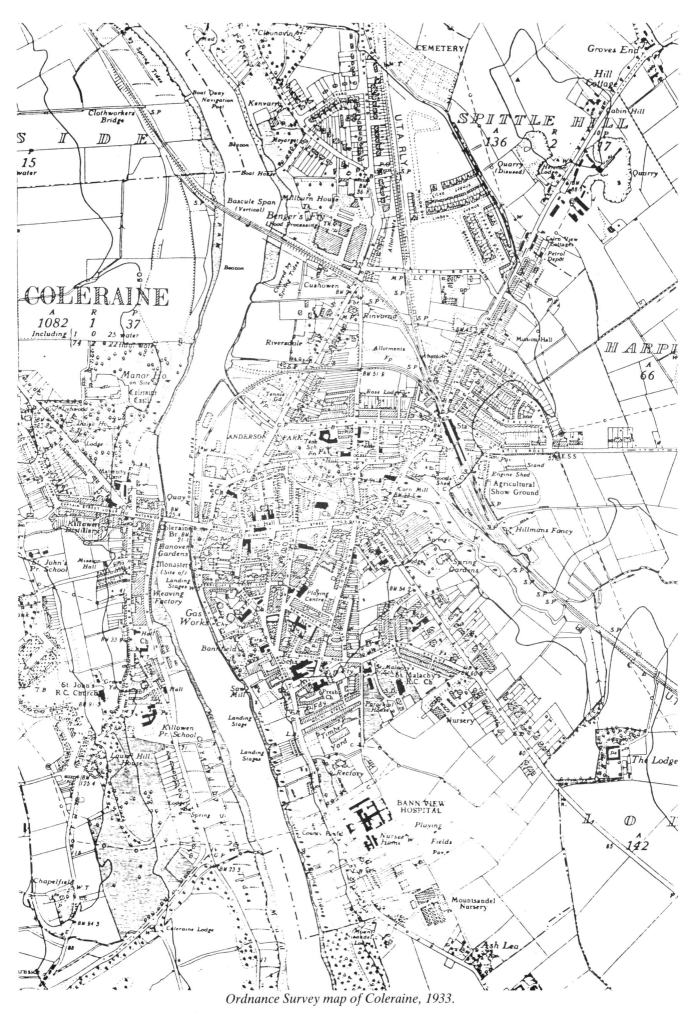

Ordnance Survey map of Coleraine, 1933.

GRAVEYARDS

Graveyards are so common that it is easy to take them for granted, but much can be learned from studying a graveyard.

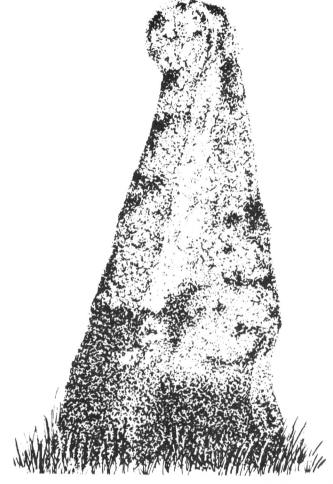

Step of a spiral stair reused as a gravestone, Corick, Co. Tyrone.

Old Graveyards

Sometimes graveyards are very old, perhaps more than 1,000 years old. Generally, old graveyards are circular or oval in shape whereas modern graveyards are usually rectangular. In an ancient graveyard there may be ruins of a church or occasionally a round tower. Sometimes, even when no stones are visible, humps and bumps in the grass can mark the outline of where a church once stood. In other cases there may be a church still in use near the graveyard. Certain kinds of stones provide clues to the age of a graveyard. Many carved crosses, for example, date back to the Early Christian period, that is, before about AD 1200.

Inscribed Gravestones

A great deal can be learned about both individuals and society in general from what is carved on a gravestone. Inscribed gravestones only became common in the seventeenth and eighteenth centuries. They can reveal a variety of information, such as the average age of death, when epidemics may have occurred and the number of babies and small children who died. This information helps to build up a picture of life expectancy, infant mortality and health in the past.

Inscriptions sometimes give details of the jobs or professions which people had. For example, a stone at Maghera graveyard, County Down, commemorates a miller, whilst a large slab carved with a chalice covers the grave of a priest on

Devenish Island in Lough Erne. In Layd churchyard, on the Antrim coast, the gravestones tell of drowned sailors and soldiers killed in foreign battles. In a corner of Bonamargy graveyard, near Ballycastle, the stones mark the graves of sailors whose bodies were washed ashore from boats sunk during the 1914-18 and 1939-45 Wars. One of them reads "A sailor, unknown stoker, Royal Navy, 30 June 1917". Sadly, some recent gravestones tell of people killed in the Troubles of the last twenty years.

An early graveyard.

Gravestones sometimes indicate the religion of the person buried there and show whether the graveyard is mixed or used by people of one particular denomination. Older gravestones belong less clearly to Catholics or Protestants than more recent stones and the oldest graveyards are usually 'mixed', serving the whole community. There are, however, some cemeteries for particular religious groups such as Quakers (in Belfast) and Jews (in Carnmoney) and Moravians (in Gracehill). As well as religion, the contrast between the rich and the poor can also be seen in graveyards. While the graves of poor people were sometimes marked with home-made wooden markers or an unmarked boulder, important families built impressive vaults, sometimes of considerable architectural splendour.

Example A

Let us take, for example, a family gravestone from Milltown Cemetery in Belfast. The marble headstone has the following inscriptions carved on it:
McMANUS

> [Marble headstone.] Erected by Teresa McManus in loving memory of her husband Richard McManus who died 4th February 1893 aged 65 years. Also his children Mary, Josephine and Annie Winifriede who died in infancy. Also our darling son Richard McManus died 6th Sept. 1894 aged 8 years.
>
> [Richard McManus was a publican at nos 53 & 55 Millfield, Belfast.)

QUESTIONS

1. How many children in the McManus family died?
2. What does 'died in infancy' mean? What does this suggest?
3. Which of the 2 people named Richard McManus died first?
4. Can you work out the age of Richard McManus, the father, when his son was born? Is this unusual?

Example B

Study the inscription on the gravestone of the Wisely family. This gravestone is in the Friar's Bush graveyard in Belfast.
WISELY

> [Celtic cross with sign of Sacred Heart, in low surround.] Erected in loving memory of Doctor Francis Joseph Wisely, Belfast, who was killed at the post of duty while attending to the sick and wounded under heavy fire at the Dardanelles, Sept. 14th 1915, aged 31 years and was buried in Alexandria, Egypt. Also James Patrick Wisely who died 1st Feby. 1908 aged 25 years. Also James Wisely who died 28th April 1909 aged 65 years. His wife Margaret Mary who died 5th Jany. 1952 aged 96 years. *A croide muir iosa dean trocaire ar an anonnaibh*.

QUESTIONS

1. How did Dr Francis Joseph Wisely die?
2. Which great war was the battle of the Dardanelles part of?
3. How did Dr Wisely come to be involved in it? On which side was he fighting?
4. Locate the Dardanelles on a map of Europe. Why was he buried in Alexandria?
5. What relation was James Patrick Wisely to Francis Joseph? Who was the elder?
6. Who was James Patrick called after? Why?
7. For how many years did Margaret Mary live after Francis Joseph was killed?
8. How do you think she would have felt when she heard the news of his heroic death in action?
9. What evidence is there to suggest that the Wisely family was of the Irish Nationalist tradition? Does this conflict with Dr Wisely's role in the British Army?

Example C

What can you deduce from this description of one particular graveyard?
The graveyard at Maghera, near Newcastle in Co. Down, is oval in shape, surrounded by a stone wall and raised high above the surrounding fields. In the graveyard is a ruined church from the 13th century and a piece of a 13th century graveslab. Just outside the walled graveyard is a Church of Ireland parish church, built in 1825, and a little distance away in the field is the stump of an Early Christian period round tower. There are several stones carved with crosses which

are quite different from the more recent gravestones — clearly much older. The graveyard is overlooked by Slieve Donard, highest peak of the Mourne Mountains, and the 6th century Saint Donard is known to have founded a church on the slopes of the Mournes. The church and round tower at Maghera are in state care and you could visit them and fill in additional details about gravestones inscriptions, vegetation, wildlife and so on. Look out for Dan Green, Miller!

PARLIAMENTARY PAPERS

The purpose of Parliamentary Papers

The evidence collected and put together in Parliamentary Papers helped the British government find out what was happening in Great Britain and Ireland in the nineteenth century. The government needed to have detailed information about important issues such as transport, education, trade and the welfare of the people. It obtained this information in a variety of ways. For example, each government department had to write regular reports of its activities. Sometimes special committees were set up to investigate a problem. Enquiries were also held during which many people were interviewed or asked to fill in questionnaires. All of this was used by the government to help it decide what policies to make. This information was also published by the government in the form of Parliamentary Papers. Because Parliamentary Papers were nearly always bound in blue covers, they became known as 'government blue books'.

These 'blue books' were sometimes read by the general public especially if they dealt with topics of local interest. Parliamentary Papers can be difficult to read because the information they contain is so detailed. They are often written in official or 'civil service' language. Because of this, it is easier to use small sections of them at a time.

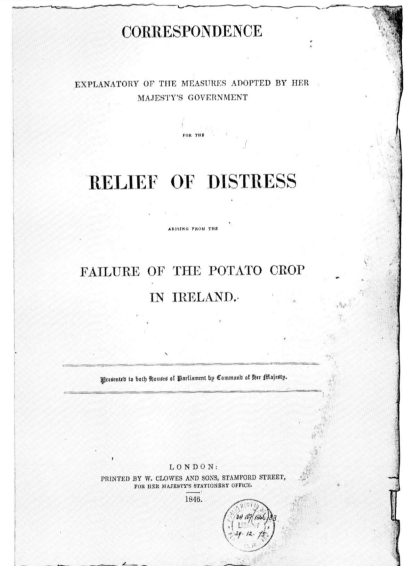

CORRESPONDENCE

EXPLANATORY OF THE MEASURES ADOPTED BY HER MAJESTY'S GOVERNMENT

FOR THE

RELIEF OF DISTRESS

ARISING FROM THE

FAILURE OF THE POTATO CROP

IN IRELAND.

Presented to both Houses of Parliament by Command of Her Majesty.

LONDON:
PRINTED BY W. CLOWES AND SONS, STAMFORD STREET,
FOR HER MAJESTY'S STATIONERY OFFICE.
1846.

Title page from a Parliamentary Paper.

How reliable are Parliamentary Papers?

Historians always ask themselves when using Parliamentary Papers — how reliable is this evidence? During an enquiry, for example, government officials travelled round Ireland, stopping in towns to take statements from local people. They may have been tempted to select only those people who could be relied on to give the point of view the government wanted to hear. Perhaps the evidence published was specially chosen to show the government in a favourable light. If this did happen, parliamentary papers may only give one side of the story.

The Famine 1845-51 Evidence from Parliamentary Papers

Parliamentary Papers can sometimes help to explain the actions of the government at a particular time. The Parliamentary Papers published during the Great Famine of 1845-51 are a good example of this.

In 1845, a mysterious disease appeared in Ireland which affected a large part of the potato crop. This was very serious as the potato was the main food available to more than half the population of Ireland (which, at that time, amounted to nearly 8½ million people). The disease did not disappear until 1851. This period is generally known as 'The Great Famine'. During these years, the government gave assistance to the Irish people in food, money and employment. Despite this, it is estimated that over 1 million people died and more than 1 million emigrated. The government has frequently been criticised for not doing enough to help the victims of the Famine.

During the Famine it was vital that the government had up-to-date information about what was happening in Ireland. On the basis of this information, they could then decide what action was necessary. The extracts below are typical of the evidence which would have been available to both the government and the public in the form of Parliamentary Papers.

CASE STUDIES

This is a letter sent to the Prime Minister, Sir Robert Peel, example B is from a local Poor Law Inspector to the Poor Law Commissioners and example C is a report from a local government official.

COMMISSARIAT.

Commissary-General HEWETSON to Sir ROBERT PEEL.

Southampton, November 5, 1845.

TRUSTING the subject of this communication will apologise for my presumption in addressing the first minister of the Crown, I beg leave most respectfully to bring under your notice, with reference to the want to be apprehended among the labouring classes in this country and Ireland, arising out of the disease so generally fatal to the potato crops, that a cheap, nutritious, and excellent substitute for the potato, viz., Indian corn meal, can be procured in great abundance in the United States of America, at a cost, in comparison with other substitutes, exceedingly low. My long residence in North America as a public officer enables me to state, with great confidence, that should Her Majesty's Government contemplate the formation of magazines in this country and Ireland for the supply, in the course of the winter, of food to the destitute classes, Indian corn meal would be the cheapest substitute for the potato, equally, if not more substantially, nutritious, and as simple in its mode of preparation. Its use in the United States is most universal among the peasantry and labouring people. Should its introduction by Her Majesty's Government into this country, for this specific purpose, be deemed expedient, by prompt and secret measures, it can be cheaply and readily purchased to any extent, and shipped from the ports of New York and Baltimore, so as to arrive here in all January, 1846 ; the arrangement would, of course, be temporary, to meet an emergency, and should such an emergency be proved, I have no hesitation in adding that Indian corn meal in every point of view, with great economy as a leading feature, is one of the best descriptions of supply that can be laid in for gratuitous distribution. Whatever prejudices, if any, may exist, as to its use as an article of food in this country, will, I should say, on trial, with simple directions for its preparation, immediately cease.

Respectfully soliciting to apologise for intruding this letter,

---

Letter from Commissariat-General Hewetson to Sir Robert Peel.

Example A

To Sir Robert Peel from Commissary — General Hewetson.
5 November 1845
"I beg leave . . . to bring to your notice the want arising out of the disease so generally fatal to the potato crops . . . and that a cheap, nutritious, and excellent substitute for the potato, namely, Indian corn meal can be procured in great abundance in the United States of America at a cost, in comparison with other substitutes, exceedingly low . . ."
Commissariat — General Hewetson·"

Example B

Report of Local Poor Law Inspector to the Poor Law Commissioners, 1849
"The majority of tenantry are, as usual, idle, reckless, lazy and improvident; many of them I could see as I passed along sitting idly smoking on the back of a ditch, without making the slightest attempt at even digging their gardens. They appear to depend on the public works or temporary relief measures to feed themselves and their family."

Example C

Edward Senior, Poor Law Inspector in Ulster
May 1848
"The distress last year was dreadful. The Northern farms are the smallest in Ireland and, besides the potato failure, the weavers were in a deplorable state. . . . Despite this, the rents were always paid and the people raised their own funds without help from the Government . . . There is a great difference between the north and the south and so it is unfair that all of Ireland is considered a diseased and corrupt body·"

QUESTIONS

Compare the three pieces of evidence.
1. What type of people wrote these reports?
2. Why do you think the views of these people were sought?
3. What attitudes to the Famine emerge from these extracts?
4. Do you think these extracts give a balanced view of the Famine as it affected ordinary people?
5. What other type of evidence could you use to find out about the effects of the Famine?

SCHOOL REGISTERS

National Schools

The National System of Education in Ireland was established in 1831-1832. Its aim was to provide schools where children could be educated almost free of charge. The schools were given grants of money as long as they accepted children from all religious denominations. A school could be established in any area if it had the support of the local clergy of the three main churches (Roman Catholic, Church of Ireland and Presbyterian). National Schools were set up throughout Ireland and by 1870 there were over 2,600 of these schools in Ulster alone.

School Registers

School registers record details about each pupil who attended a National School. Each pupil was given a number when he or she entered the school. This number, the pupil's name, age (or sometimes date of birth), religion, home address, and father's occupation was recorded in the school registers. The register also recorded the subjects they studied and what level of reading book they had progressed to. There was also a column in which teachers could record why pupils left school. This sometimes provided details of what the pupils did after they left. The information in school registers, therefore, allows us to build up a picture of what type of children attended school and how children were educated in the 19th century.

EXAMINE THE EXTRACT FROM A TYPICAL 19th CENTURY SCHOOL REGISTER ON PAGE OPPOSITE

QUESTIONS

1. How could you tell that there were separate schools for boys and girls?
2. How many different religious denominations were represented at this school?
3. What does 'non-denominational' mean?
4. Which boy's religion is unusual? What do you think it means?
5. Why are there 2 Alex Gibsons? How can you tell that the 2 entries refer to the same boy? What is different about the second entry?
6. Which occupations make you think that the school could be situated near the coast?
7. Why do you think that Edward Boyle (No. 7 on the list) only joined school when he was aged 13¼?
8. Study the column on the extreme right. At what age did pupils appear to leave school to take up a job?
9. How are the registers similar to Census records (see pages 42-44)?
10. List as many things as possible which historians can learn from school registers?

Religious Denominations are marked thus—
E.C. Established Church.
R.C. Roman Catholic.
Pres. Presbyterian.
Dis. Dissenter.

Register of ____________ National School.

Industrial Instruction in Girls' Schools thus:—
Col. (a) Elementary Sewing.
" (b) Making bibs, frocks, shirts, &c.
" (c) Sewed Muslin Work and Embroidery.
Col. (d) Plain Knitting.
" (e) Fancy Knitting, Netting, and Crochet Work.
" (f) Cutting out.

Number in former Register.	Register Number.	Date of Entrance. 1855.	Pupils' Names.	Age of Pupil.	Religious Denomination.	Residence.	Occupation, or Means of Living of Parents.	Reading Books. 1.	2	Sequels.	3	4.	5.	Sacred Poetry.	Scripture Lessons.	Grammar. Parts of Speech.	Parsing and Syntax.	Derivation.	Composition.	Geography. Maps only.	Local and Descriptive.	Physical and Mathematical.
54	1	Jan. 8	James Murray	7½	R.C.	Tubberclare	Farmer		1/55	9/55										1/55		
66	2	" "	~~Alex. Gibson~~	13	Pres.	47, John-st. Clonmel	Draper					1/55		1/55	1/55		1/55	1/55			1/55	6/55
213	3	" "	John Cahill	8¼	R.C.	Killusty	Tailor			1/55	6/55					1/55	6/55	6/55			6/55	
	4	" "	Henry Thomson	8½	E.C.	Gurteen	LandSteward	1/55	7/55	12/55				7/55	12/55	7/55		•		1/55		
	5	" "	~~Peter Masterson~~	6¾	R.C.	Mardyke	Distiller		1/55	4/55	11/55					1/55	8/55	11/55		1/55	12/56	
	6	" "	Eugene O'Reilly	5¼	R.C.	Ballyfarsoon	Widow–Farmer	1/55	8/55							8/55				1/55		
	7	" "	Edward Doyle	13¼	R.C.	Raheen	Blacksmith				1/55 6–55	(4/55) 9–55	2/56				1/55	1/55	2/56		1/55 6–55	(4/55) 9–55
	69	Feb. 19	Florence M'Carthy	6	R.C.	Slievavadaragh	Fisherman	2/55	12/55							12/55				2/55		
	124	Sept. 10	~~Hugh Maloney~~	14	R.C.	Kilbride	Schoolmaster					9/55	2/56				9/55	9/55	2/56		9/55	9/55
	125	" "	Patrick Dunne	9½	R.C.	Castleraghan	Weaver	9/55	12/55	4/56						12/55				9/55		
	147	1856 Jan. 7	Henry M'Afee	11	Dis.	Miltown	Sailor				1/56	8/56		1/56	1/56		1/56	8/56			1/56	8/56
	148/2	" 28	Alex. Gibson	14	Pres.	123, Main-st. Clonmel	Draper					1/56	4/56		1/56		1/56	1/56	4/56		1/56	1/56

Register Number.	Arithmetic. Tables only.	Notation and Simple Rules.	Compound Rules.	Proportion to Practice.	Practice and above.	Mental.	Writing. On Slates.	On Paper.	From Dictation.	Extra Branches. British Poets.	Mensuration. (a.)	Geometry. (b.)	Algebra. (c.)	Bookkeeping.	Trigonometry. (d.)	Reasoning. (e.)	Agriculture.	Navigation. (f.)	Music.	Drawing.	Physical and Applied Science.	Date on which Pupil's Name was Struck off Roll and Register.	Cause of Withdrawal, and Destination of Pupil.
1		1/55	9/55				1/55	3/55	9/55										1/55				
2					1/55	1/55		1/55	1/55	1/55	6/55	6/55	8/55	6/55			1/55		1/55	1/55		17–11/'55	Illness.
3		1/55	3/55	8/55		6/55		1/55	3/55										1/55	6/55			
4	1/55	6/55	3/56				5/55	9/55	12/55										7/55				
5		1/55	3/55	2/56		11/55		1/55	4/55										1/55	11/55		19–1/'56	Clerk in a timber-yard.
6	1/55	6/55					4/55	8/55											1/55	1/55			
7			6–55	(1/55) 7–55	9/55	1/55		1/55	1/55	(4/55) 9–55	9/55	9/55	12/55	9/55		2/56	(4/55) 9–55		1/55	1/55	2/56		
69	2/55	12/55					2/55	12/55											12/55				
124					9/55	9/55		9/55	9/55	9/55	9/55	9/55	12/55	9/55		2/56	9/55		9/55	9/55	2/56	28–6/'56	Apprenticed to a Carpenter.
125	9/55	12/55	7/56				9/55	12/55	10/56										12/55				
147				1/56	8/56	1/56		1/56	1/56	1/56	8/56	8/56	10/56	8/56			8/56		1/56	1/56			
148/2					1/56	1/56		1/56	1/56	1/56	1/56	1/56	3/56	1/56		4/56	1/56		1/56	1/56	4/56		

Directions for keeping the Register, and which Teachers are required to strictly observe.

1. *Object of the Register.*—The Register is by far the most important of the School records, and is to the educationist what the *Ledger* is to the mercantile man. Whilst the Rolls show the daily attendance of each child individually, and the Report Book exhibits the daily numerical strength of the School in classes and also collectively, *the object of the Register is to show the personal school-history of each Pupil* that is admitted; his age at entrance, religious persuasion, residence, social position as indicated by his parents' occupation or means of living, his attainments at entrance, his subsequent proficiency in the several branches of the course of instruction, the date of his withdrawal and the cause, and his destination. In fact, it is from the Registers of our Schools, combined and collated with the Report Books and Class Rolls, that the leading data of the problem of National Education must be collected, and hence the great importance attached to the correct keeping of these records, and the censure and punishment which the Commissioners invariably inflict for any neglect in this respect on the part of Teachers.

2. *Registration.*—When a Child presents himself for admission to the School, it is most desirable that he should be accompanied by either parent, the father if possible; or if not by a parent, then by an elder brother or sister, a grandparent, uncle, aunt, or in the case of an orphan, by his nearest natural or other legal guardian. It is from one of these that the *Religious Denomination* of the Child must be ascertained, and when once registered it must not be changed on the Register except on the application of the parent, or of such natural or other guardian, as may be *legally authorized* to direct such a change. From the Parents also the Teacher can best obtain *reliable* information as to the Pupil's exact age.

3. *Classification.*—If possible all admissions should take place on Mondays only, and *immediately on the Pupil's entrance* the first eight columns of the Register in reference to him should *at once* be filled up as above indicated. The Teacher should then proceed to examine carefully the Pupil, *according to the scale of Classification laid down in the School Programme*, and enter in what class, branches, &c., he is fit to be placed, *quite irrespective of what he may have been learning when last in this or any other School*, and being wholly guided by the proficiency required by the Programme for each class. Thus *James Murray* on examination was found fit to read Second Book, and 1/55 shows that he commenced this Book in the 1st Month (January), of the year 1855, and his attainments on entrance in Grammar, Geography, Arithmetic, and Writing are similarly indicated by the headings of the columns in the Classification Table, in which 1/55 stands after his name.

4. *Promotion or Depression.*—The *proficiency* of the Pupils should be inquired into every *Saturday*, in order that the progress of each child from branch to branch, or from the lower to the higher divisions of a subject, may be *posted* in the Register; thus 9/55 *James Murray* commenced to write on paper, and 9/55 he was promoted into Sequel Class, into the Compound Rules of Arithmetic, and commenced to write from Dictation. When a circle is drawn with the pen round the date at which a subject was commenced, as in the case of *Edward Doyle*, it indicates that from inattention, or from extreme dulness, or from irregular attendance, although not wholly absent for 13 consecutive weeks, the Pupil was *depressed*, or put back to a lower class, as in Reading from 4th to 3rd Book, that he ceased to read the British Poets, and further that he was removed from the Senior to the Junior Class in Geography. If the Pupil be again re-admitted to these Classes, the date is to be entered in the corresponding columns under the circle, in the manner indicated in the case of *Edward Doyle*, who was re-admitted to his former Classes in September, 1855.

NEWSPAPERS

In the twentieth century, people have become very used to newspapers as an everyday item, informing us about what is happening locally, nationally and internationally. A newspaper may be delivered or brought into your house every day or at weekends. Modern newspapers present news in a variety of ways which include headline news about major events, articles by on-the-spot reporters and up-to-date photographs. They also include editorial comments, sports news, crosswords, horoscopes and information on television and radio programmes.

Newspapers in the 18th Century

Eighteenth and nineteenth century newspapers were very different in style and content from today's newspapers but are just as valuable as evidence. A typical newspaper contained a large number of advertisements and public notices with news items often only starting on the second page. Local news reports were mainly about road building, court cases, the local gentry and the latest fashions. Newspapers also included long extracts from parliamentary debates, events in London and major events in foreign countries, especially wars. All of this would have been written in small print with no photographs to break up the text. Since only well-educated people could read, it was often the custom for a local person to read out extracts to groups of people wherever they met — in houses, inns, at markets or any other local gathering points. There were no public libraries.

Ireland has the oldest surviving newspaper in Europe. The *Belfast News Letter* has been in continuous existence, without a break, since it was started in 1737. There are not many copies available for the first few years but, from the early 1750s, the *Belfast News Letter* is an important source of information for historians. It was published twice a week and sold many copies throughout Ulster. The most complete set of copies is in The Linen Hall Library in Belfast.

You can obtain a good deal of historical information from a study of the contents of newspapers, but there are problems involved. Many early papers lack a coherent lay-out and have a rather haphazard organisation. It is often difficult, therefore, to find easily what you are looking for. There may be problems over the tightly packed layout, the unfamiliar words and the old-fashioned language. You will see some of these problems for yourself in some of the extracts we are going to consider.

One of the most regular items in Irish newspapers were notices about emigration. The extract below would have been eagerly read, especially by friends of the people who sent this letter from America to the *Belfast News Letter*.

Example A Belfast News Letter 14-17 June 1774

We whose names are hereunto subscribed, together with all the passengers on board, think it necessary to acquaint our friends, and the Publick in general, of the generous, friendly and good natured behaviour of Capt William Reed in the ship Waddell, to us all. Nor must we in gratitude forget to do justice to the owners who laid in provisions and water of a sufficient quantity . . .

Now, as Capt Reed intends to come in the Passenger Trade, we earnestly wish and desire that such of our friends as are minded to embark for the New World may lay hold of so favourable an opportunity as soon as is convenient, as the ship Waddell is in every way compleat and stout and properly fitted for the passenger trade.

QUESTIONS

1. How is the captain described?
2. What it meant by 'the New World'?
3. Why do you think the people who travelled on the ship signed the letter:
   (a) they were relieved to get across the Atlantic safely
   (b) they wanted their friends in Ireland to join them
   (c) they were glad to get off the ship?
4. If you read this in 1774, would you be tempted to emigrate?

There was no paid or regular police force in the 18th and some of the 19th century. Notices in the newspapers alerted people to stolen goods and rewards were even offered by local inhabitants who thought it was in their interest to capture the suspects.

Example B Northern Star 6-10 March 1797

100 GUINEAS REWARD

Whereas on Tuesday morning of the 7th, the Roman Catholic Chapel of Tullysaran in County Armagh was discovered to be on fire and was in the short time after entirely consumed. And whereas there is every reason to believe that the said chapel was wilfully and maliciously set on fire by some person or persons unknown. Now we, the undersigned inhabitants of Armagh and in this vicinity, wholly in abhorrence about the detestable proceedings of this nature, which have so long disgraced some parts of this country, do promise to pay the sum of one hundred guineas, in proportion to the sums annexed to our respective names, as reward to any person or persons who shall in 6 calendar months from this date, discover and prosecute to conviction the perpetrators of the above atrocious action.

Arthur J M'Can Esq	£11. 7s.6d.	Alexander Prentice	£3.8s.3d.
Sovereign of Armagh		James Stewart	£3.8s.3d.
Joshua M'Geough Esq	£5.13s.9d.	George Murry	£3.8s.3d.
Robert Livingston Esq	£5.13s.9d.	Thomas Greer	£3.8s.3d.
Rev James A Hamilton	£5.13s.9d.	John Prentice	£2.5s.6d.
Rev Thomas Carpindale	£5.13s.9d.	John Bleakley	£2.5s.6d.
Rev Daniel Kelly	£5.13s.9d.	Thomas Bleakley	£2.5s.6d.
Edward Quinn	£5.13s.9d.	Thomas Walsh	£2.5s.6d.
Richard Whittington	£5.13s.9d.	William Andrews	£2.5s.6d.

QUESTIONS

1. Why was such a reward offered in the *Northern Star*?
2. What evidence is there that many Protestants signed this reward notice?
3. What is unusual about this and what does it tell about this period in Ulster?
4. FIND OUT more about the United Irishmen.

Newspapers in the 19th Century

One of the features that sometimes appeared in 18th century newspapers and which became more common in 19th century newspapers were accounts of people who were tried in local courts.

Example C Belfast Newsletter Extracts 1804-12

13 April 1804 *Downpatrick Assizes:* Margaret Connolly alias Connaught Peg was found guilty as a vagabond and sentenced to transportation unless she should give security for her future good behaviour.

James Finlay who had been tried by a Court Martial at Newtownards in the County of Down for treason committed by him in the Rebellion of 1798 and sentenced to be transported to Botany Bay for 14 years was brought to trial for returning to Ireland. He was ordered to be pilloried and afterwards to be transported to Botany Bay for life.

24 July 1812 *Armagh Assizes 20 July*: William Gormel, James Smith alias Daly and Elizabeth Armstrong for stealing four pieces of linen cloth from the bleach green of Messrs. Patrick & John Robinson near Keady on the night of the 13th April 1812. William Gormel and Elizabeth Armstrong guilty. James Smith not guilty.

William Gormel to be transported for several years and Elizabeth Armstrong to be burned in the hand and imprisoned for six months.

James Boylan a boy apparently about 12 or 13 years of age for picking the pocket of James Quinn in the market of Newtownhamilton. Guilty; to be transported for seven years.

QUESTIONS

1. List the crimes which led to people being transported?
2. Why were these people sent so far away?
3. What are the STRENGTHS and WEAKNESSES of these newspaper details in giving evidence about attitudes to law-breaking in the 19th century?
4. *'These details were printed by newspapers as a means of maintaining law and order in the public interest'*. Give reasons to AGREE or DISAGREE with the statement.

Newspaper Advertisements

Newspapers in the 19th century also allowed the growing number of shops to advertise goods available for sale. More and more notices for the sale of goods appeared in newspapers and, very often, the goods on sale were of a much more sophisticated kind than had been available only a few years before. Jewellery and watches, ladies' and gentlemen's clothes, often made overseas, were brought to the public's attention in newspaper advertisements. The advertisement on p.41 taken from the *Banner of Ulster* of 12 April 1850, sets out a range of goods that had arrived in Belfast shops and which would attract the interest of the population. Read the advertisements and answer the questions as if you were doing some research on how people lived in the middle of the nineteenth century in Belfast.

THE BANNER OF ULSTER, FRIDAY, APRIL 12, 1850.

NOTICE.

THE UNDERSIGNED beg respectfully to announce that the business carried on by the late Firm of J. & D. LINDSAY & CO. will in future be conducted by them, in all its Departments, under the Firm of LINDSAY, BROTHERS.

Belfast, 1st April, 1850.

JAMES LINDSAY.
THOMAS G. LINDSAY.
ROBERT LINDSAY.

Useful, Elegant, and Economical Birth-day and Wedding Presents,

AT MACARTNEY'S,

Jeweller, Watchmaker, and Optician,
6, DONEGALL PLACE, BELFAST.

Papier Mache.

Exquisitely Decorated and highly Embellished Victoria, Regency, and Cottage DESKS; Venetian, Egyptian, and Gothic WORK-BOXES, with Solid Silver Fittings.
ALBUMS, PORTFOLIOS, WORK-TABLES, Devotional CHAIRS, SCREENS, &c., with Persian, Pearl, and Oil PAINTINGS.
N.B.—Ladies' Fancy Work Mounted as Screens. Designs and estimates furnished.

Jewellery.

Many New and Rare Designs, in BRACELETS, BROOCHES, CHAINS, NECKLETS, at much lower prices than usually charged.

Ladies Fine Gold Rings, set with Pearls, — 14s, 16s, 18s
Do. do. do. set with Pearls, Rubies, and Emeralds,— 21s, 28s, 30s
Ladies Fine Gold Rings, set with Rubies, Emeralds, and Brilliants,— 42s, 63s, 84s
Brilliant Single Stone and Half-hoop Rings, of the rarest lustre, — 84s to £20
Gentlemen's Fine Gold Signet Rings, — 12s to 55s
Stone Seal Engravings artistically executed.
Ladies' old Jewellery Remodelled.
Hair Bracelets and Chains elegantly made to order.

Watches.

A large and superior Stock of First-Class London and Geneva Gold and Silver WATCHES, with all the modern improvements, at unusually low prices.

Silver Watches, from — £3 3 0
Gold do. do. — 5 15 0
Excellent Second-hand Silver WATCHES, suitable for Servants, £1 10s each.

Genuine Sheffield and Patent Electro-Plated Ware.

DINNER FORKS and TABLE SPOONS, 48s per dozen; DESSERTS, 42s per ditto. All A1 quality. Cash—discount 10 per cent.

Spectacles and Eye Glasses to suit all Sights and Ages.

Gold Spectacles — 21s per pair.
Steel do. — 3s —
Cataract do. — 3s —

A Variety of British and Foreign Fancy Goods.

FANS, Patent SCENT BOTTLES, CARD and NETTING BOXES, LADIES' COMPANIONS (at home and abroad), TICKET CASES, &c.

REPAIRING in all the Departments. Old Gold, Silver, or Jewels taken in Exchange. Bog Oak Work made in the Establishment.

HASLETT & FRAZER

BEG to intimate that they are DAILY RECEIVING their SPRING and SUMMER STOCK of **PLAIN AND FANCY WOOLLENDRAPERY,** PARIS AND LONDON VESTINGS, HATS, &c., &c., From the first Manufacturers, purchased within the last fortnight.

21, HIGH STREET, April 4, 1850.

EXTENSION OF PREMISES.

OPENING OF THE NEW WAREROOMS,

AT THE PANTECHNETHECA.

JOHN G. M'GEE AND COMPANY

RESPECTFULLY ANNOUNCE THAT THEIR NEW WAREROOMS ARE NOW OPEN, AND CONTAIN

AN EXTENSIVE AND FASHIONABLE STOCK OF EVERY NOVELTY, FOR GENTLEMEN'S DRESS,

Which has been produced, this season, in the French and English markets, having been personally selected, during the last fortnight, by one of the Firm, from the most celebrated Manufacturers of Elbeuf, Paris, London, and the West of England.

NEW ARRIVALS OF SPRING GOODS.

MOSES & CO. respectfully intimate to the Gentry and Inhabitants of Belfast, that they have now received a Splendid Assortment of NEW GOODS for the Season, in which will be found some of the most recent designs, in

FRENCH DOESKINS FOR TROUSERS,

AN ARTICLE MUCH ADMIRED FOR ELASTICITY AND BEAUTY OF TEXTURE; ALSO, A MAGNIFICENT SUPPLY OF

LONDON AND FRENCH VESTINGS,

OF THE MOST BEAUTIFUL PATTERNS THE SEASON HAS PRESENTED;

NEW MATERIALS FOR COATS, IN BRITANNIA, BERLINS, AND LETE CLOTHS,

ALL OF WHICH WILL BE MADE UP IN A SUPERIOR MANNER BY EFFICIENT WORKMEN; A LARGE STOCK OF

LONDON AND FRENCH HATS,

IN THE NEWEST AND MOST FASHIONABLE SHAPES;

Servants' Liveries, &c.

MOSES AND COMPANY,

TAILORS, DRAPERS, CLOTHIERS, HATTERS, &c.,
8, DONEGALL PLACE.

Exhibition of the Collection of the Belfast Government School of Design,

AS DISPLAYED AT THE INAUGURATION, ON THE 10TH INST.

OPEN to the Public, on FRIDAY, and SATURDAY, from TWELVE till THREE, P.M.; on the Evening of FRIDAY, from SEVEN till TEN; and on SATURDAY Evening from SIX till NINE.
Admission on Friday till Three o'clock, Sixpence each; and from Three o'clock on Friday and on Saturday, at the above-named hours, for the Working Classes, at Twopence. The Pupils of the School will be admitted free of charge.

(By order),
C. BESSEL, Assistant-Secretary.
Government School of Design, 11th April, 1850.

Reduction in Price of Alabaster,

AT THE EXTENSIVE ROMAN CEMENT AND ALABASTER WORKS OF JOHN CUDDY.

JOHN CUDDY begs to inform the Trade that, having now completed extensive additions to his Works, and made important improvements, he is now in a position to execute all orders sent him with despatch, and at a lower price than it can be made for by any other house. The quality of his Alabaster and Roman Cement is so well known as to be the means of making his Manufactory the most extensive in the kingdom.

Roman Cement, Alabaster, and Gypsum Mills, Upper Church Lane; Office, 42, Church Lane.
Belfast, 8th April, 1850.

QUESTIONS

1. List 10 items for sale in Belfast in April 1850.
2. What do these adverts tell us about life in Belfast in 1850?
3. How would a newspaper like *The Banner of Ulster* be useful to an historian?
4. What two other sources might an historian need to consult to provide accurate details about life in Belfast and Ulster in the 1850s? Give reasons for your choices.

CENSUS RETURNS

The Census of Ireland: 1901 Household Return.

What are Census Returns?

Every household is required by the government to fill in a census form once every 10 years. Someone in your house will have filled in a census form for your family at one time. These forms are known as HOUSEHOLD RETURNS because they collect information on each household in the country. The head of the household is asked to give details on all of the people staying in that house on a certain day. These details include the name, age, occupation and religion of the occupants. This information is confidential and cannot be seen by other members of the public for 100 years.*

The government uses the details provided in the household returns to obtain information about groups within the population. For example, they can calculate the number of males and females there are in the country and their ages, the number of schoolchildren, whether people are single, married, divorced or widowed, etc. This statistical information is very valuable and is put together by the government into PRINTED REPORTS. These show how the population is changing. The government can use this information to estimate, for example, how many schools or houses will be required in the next 10 years. The printed reports can be seen by the public because they do not reveal information about individuals.

The value of Census Returns

Just as the census returns provide vital information to help the government decide on future policies, they can also help researchers find out about the past — perhaps the history of a particular family or about certain groups within that society. A historian, for example, could compare the statistics in a recent printed report with those in an earlier one to see how the population has changed. The details about individual families found in the household returns will also be of great interest to future historians when they become available after a hundred years.

CASE STUDIES

Below are extracts from the 1861 printed report (example A) and the 1901 and 1911 household returns (examples B & C).

*Censuses for the years before 1921 are held in the National Archives in Dublin. They can be consulted by the public.

Example A: A Printed Return

Parishes, Townlands, and Towns.	Area.	Population					Houses					
		In 1841. Persons.	In 1851. Persons.	In 1861. Males.	Females.	Total.	In 1841. Number.	In 1851. Number.	In 1861. In-habited.	Unin-habited.	Build-ing.	Total.
	A. R. P.											
Boho Parish, part of:												
Acres,	11 2 29	10	12	3	2	5	2	2	1	.	.	1
Aghaherrish,	277 0 1	177	89	37	31	68	30	21	16	1	.	17
Aghanaglack,	1,345 0 19	121	106	43	47	90	21	17	15	.	.	15
Agho,	916 0 8	185	172	77	72	149	27	26	26	.	.	26
Carn,	122 3 14	10	16	11	7	18	2	4	2	1	.	3
Coolarkan,	573 2 27	78	79	32	21	53	18	15	10	1	.	11
Dooletter,	512 2 34	37	26	14	20	34	7	5	7	.	.	7
Drumboy,	166 0 17	99	54	19	28	47	20	15	12	1	.	13
Drumgamph,	99 1 31	53	35	16	19	35	9	6	6	.	.	6
Drumlirk, Lower,	77 2 31	43	33	15	18	33	8	8	5	.	.	5
Drumlirk, Upper,	70 3 27	38	31	11	10	21	6	4	4	.	.	4
Drummacoorin,	126 0 10	42	33	13	17	30	8	9	7	.	.	7
Gortgall,	624 3 23	82	82	21	18	39	13	9	6	2	.	8
Kilnamaddoo,	179 0 22	65	45	20	14	34	12	7	8	.	.	8
Legnagay Beg,	1,153 0 18	56	54	19	16	35	11	8	4	.	.	4
Legnagay More,	98 3 13	50	12	14	9	23	8	1	4	1	.	5
Lesky,	196 2 3	89	58	20	29	49	17	11	9	.	.	9
Ross,	156 0 35	59	42	27	33	60	9	7	9	.	.	9
Stralahan,	555 0 14	24	19	9	13	22	5	4	5	.	.	5
Tievebunnan,	616 2 37	60	69	41	36	77	11	12	12	.	.	12
Tobradan,	151 1 17	123	60	23	21	44	21	12	9	1	.	10
Toneel, South,	36 2 0	21	13	7	9	16	4	3	3	.	.	3
Treel,	325 3 37	36	26	14	11	25	6	4	5	1	.	6
Tullygerravra,	481 0 3	75	79	35	26	61	12	12	10	.	.	10
Tullyholvin, Lower,	19 1 9	27	8	9	5	14	5	2	2	.	.	2
Tullyholvin, Upper,	17 0 23	15	19	5	11	16	4	3	2	.	.	2
Total, (a)	8,911 0 17	1,675	1,222	555	543	1,098	296	227	199	9	.	208

This is an extract from the 1861 printed census return. It provides information on the Boho Parish in County Fermanagh. Boho Parish is, in turn, subdivided into townlands and towns. From this table we are able to find out much information about the population of each of these townlands not only in 1861, but also in 1841 and 1851. The table also tells us how many houses were in each townland and the value of the land in this area.

QUESTIONS

1. What is the name of the largest townland in Boho Parish?
2. Make a table or barchart of the changes in population between 1841 and 1861. Why do you think these changes have taken place?

Example B: A Household Return

Census of Ireland, 1901

Name	Relation to Head of Family	Religion	Education	Age	Sex	Profession	Marriage	Where Born
Alexander, Huxley	Head of Family	Presbyterian	Cannot read or write	66	M	Agricultural labourer	Married	Holywood, Co. Down
Arabella, Huxley	Wife	Roman Catholic	Read and write	65	F		Married	Holywood, Co. Down
Eliza, Huxley	Daughter	Roman Catholic	Read and write	40	F	Labourer	Not married	Holywood, Co. Down
Alexander, Huxley	Son	Roman Catholic	Cannot read or write	32	M	Gardener	Widower	Holywood, Co. Down
William, Huxley	Son	Roman Catholic	Read and write	26	M	Plasterer	Not married	Holywood, Co. Down
Alexander, Huxley	Grandson	Roman Catholic	Cannot read	5	M	Scholar	Not married	Holywood, Co. Down
Arabella, Huxley	Grand-daughter	Roman Catholic	Read only	8	F	Scholar	Not married	Holywood, Co. Down

This is the return of a family from Holywood, County Down in the 1901 Census. Alexander Huxley, the head of the family, is a Presbyterian. As you can see, his wife, children and grandchildren are Roman Catholic. Alexander's son and grandson have the same first name. It was a very common tradition in Ireland for the father's name to be passed on to his children or grandchildren. Alexander is an agricultural labourer. He was unable to read or write. His son aged 32 was also illiterate. It is interesting to note that the young children who attended school are referred to as 'scholars'.

QUESTIONS

1. Construct a simple family tree for the Huxley family.
2. Look at the columns for 'name' and 'surname'. Why are there 3 people named Alexander Huxley. What does this tell you about how children got their names in the past?
3. Look at the column with the heading 'Relation to Head of the Family'. How many generations can you detect? How many generations are there in your own home?
4. Look at the column 'Education'. Which of Alexander and Arabella Huxley's 3 children could not read or write? Why do you think this was?
5. Look at the 'Marriage' column. Only one of Alexander and Arabella's children is married. Which one? Can you say from this who is the father of the 2 children on the form, Alexander and Arabella?
6. Look at the 'Where Born' column. Can you give a reason why young Arabella was born in Ballycastle and her brother in Holywood?
7. Look at the 'Profession' column. What is a scholar?
8. Why do you think Alexander signed his name with an 'X'?
9. Construct an imaginary census return for the Huxley family in 1911.

Example C: Household Return 1911

Census of Ireland, 1911

Name	Relation to Head of Family	Religion	Education	Age	Sex	Profession	Marriage	Where Born
Patrick Ryan	Head of Family	Roman Catholic	Write and read	54	M	Farmer	Married	Tipperary
Margaret Ryan	Wife	Roman Catholic	Read and write	41	F		Married	Tipperary
William Ryan	Son	Roman Catholic	Cannot read	5	M	Scholar	Single	Tipperary
James Ryan	Son	Roman Catholic	Cannot read	4	M	Scholar	Single	Tipperary
Patrick Ryan	Son	Roman Catholic	Cannot read	2	M		Single	Tipperary
Michael Ryan	Son	Roman Catholic	Cannot read	3 mth	M		Single	Tipperary
Margaret Ryan	Mother	Roman Catholic	Read	75	F	Old Age Pensioner	Widow	Limerick
Michael Ryan	Servant	Roman Catholic	Read	20	M	Farm servant	Single	Tipperary

QUESTIONS

1. From the above information construct a family tree for the Ryan family.
2. What were the ages of Patrick and Margaret when they married?
3. How many children belong to Patrick and his wife?
4. Who is not related to the family in the house? Why do you think he is staying with them?
5. What does this census return tell us about the way people lived together in 1911?

GLOSSARY

census — official record of population
manuscript — written by hand
townland — a small area of land (usually in the countryside)
valuation — the estimated value of an area of land
illiterate — not able to read or write

PHOTOGRAPHS

A photograph is an instant and lasting pictorial record of an event. A good photograph can capture the atmosphere and detail of the past better than a lengthy description. Photographs allow us to see for ourselves what life may have been like at a particular place and time. Photographs are, therefore, invaluable pieces of evidence for historians in helping to piece together accurate views of the past.

Staged Photographs

i. Photography was invented in 1839. Before the invention of photography, people had to rely upon drawings, paintings and engravings. Look at A and B which show one stage in the process of flax being turned into linen cloth.

Flax taken from the dam, by W. Hincks (A).

Flax taken from the dam, by W. A. Green (B).

A was drawn by William Hincks in 1783 to show how flax was taken from the dam where it had been soaking for 10-14 days. B is a photograph taken by William A. Green in the 1920s showing the same process. Which picture gives a better idea of what the job was like for the workers? Why do you think William Hincks painted such a pretty picture?

ii. While photographs are more accurate than drawings it is still necessary to be wary of when, where and why they were taken.

Women from Clogher Valley (C).

Model in London Department Store (D).

Compare the clothing worn by the woman in photograph C (taken in the Clogher Valley in 1907) with that in photograph D. The woman in the second photograph was demonstrating Irish embroidery at a department store in London in 1917. She is dressed as people in London imagined an 'Irish colleen' would dress. How does the 'costume' in photograph D differ from the real thing?

Alexander Findlay's son (E).

iii. Look at photograph E taken around 1880. The little boy is dressed as 'Little Lord Fauntleroy' — the hero of a successful romantic novel of the time. This photograph was taken in a studio with a background made to look like the little lord's estate. The boy was, however, the son of the Belfast soap manufacturer, Alexander Finlay, who, although wealthy, was certainly not an aristocrat. Why do you think Mr. Finlay had this photograph taken of his child dressed in this way?

Documentary Photographs

The sort of photograph which can usually be taken at face value is the documentary photograph. A documentary photograph is usually taken at the request of companies who wish to keep a record of their work. In Ulster the main industries were photographed in detail by respected photographers such as R. J. Welch and W. A. Green. Harland & Wolff, for example, asked Mr. Welch to photograph the building of ships at their yard at Queen's Island.

Photograph F is one of the photographs which he took. It shows the ceiling of a room on a passenger liner built in 1897. Ships rarely survive for very long even if they don't sink, like the Titanic! Without such photographs as this, if would be difficult for us to imagine the size and magnificence of the great ocean liners built by Harland and Wolff. What was the purpose of this particular documentary photograph?

Interior of passenger liner built in Belfast (F).

How reliable are photographs as evidence?

The previous examples show that, while photographs can be very useful, it is helpful to know when or why they were taken. A camera faithfully records all that is put in front of it, but one must remember that it is the photographer who has chosen what to photograph. It is necessary, therefore, to think about why the photograph was taken. Photographs can sometimes be changed even after they have been taken, by altering the negative.

Photographs, especially of people at work, cannot convey working conditions such as noise, smell or temperature. Sometimes it is difficult to establish a precise date for a photograph. People and places in photographs can be difficult to identify. Photographs, therefore, need to be used along with other evidence such as oral history, newspaper accounts etc. When they are used like this, they can provide a unique flavour of the past.

N.B. All photographs used are in the collections of the Ulster Folk and Transport Museum.

POSTERS

Posters are notices displayed in public places to convey information to passers-by. In the past, posters were often used to announce important news. In local towns and villages, for example, they advertised when fairs, markets or local elections were to be held. Sometimes they were a means of communicating urgent information, such as the possible outbreak of disease, advising people how they might protect themselves.

Posters were also used to announce important national events, such as the outbreak of war. These were issued by the government and were designed to appeal to people's emotions. For example, during the First World War recruitment posters encouraged young men to join the army by portraying soldiers as heroic and patriotic.

Some employers used posters to inform their workforce about rules and regulations such as hours of work, meal breaks, holidays and what rights they had if they fell sick.

**Poster A:
A poster warning
about cholera**

One of the most feared diseases in the nineteenth century was cholera. It could spread quickly, affect an entire area and was difficult to control. There was no proven cure for it. In the early 1830s, outbreaks of cholera were reported from several parts of Ireland. This poster was the most effective way of warning the inhabitants of Ahoghill, County Antrim, about the arrival of the disease and advising them how to avoid being affected by it.

QUESTIONS

1. Study the first paragraph of the poster. What is meant by 'gratuitous' and how does this show that the doctors in the parish of Ahoghill were taking the threat of cholera very seriously?
2. Which part of the body does the disease affect most?
3. How can you tell that the disease affects people very quickly and sometimes kills them within hours?
4. What can you deduce from the last paragraph about:
   (a) the usual state of cleanliness to be found in houses?
   (b) what people slept on?
5. What does 'intemperance in the use of ardent spirits' mean? Why do you think the Board of Health felt it necessary to state this?
6. If you were an historian researching the history of medicine in Ireland in the nineteenth century, what would this document tell you about:
   (a) the knowledge of doctors about cholera?
   (b) the awareness of the public of the importance of hygiene?

**Poster B:
National events —
First World War**

QUESTIONS

1. Many posters do not have a date on them. Give a date for this source.
2. The poster says 'We must have more men'. Who does 'we' refer to?
3. How would this poster appeal to people's patriotism?
4. This poster was put up in Ballymoney, Co. Antrim. Was it produced there?
   Do you think this poster would have been displayed:
   (a) only in Ballymoney
   (b) in Ballymoney and London
   (c) throughout the British Isles?

5. What impression of being a soldier do you get from this picture:
   (a) soldiers are well dressed
   (b) soldiers are brave
   (c) soldiers are patriotic
   (d) anyone who is not a soldier is not patriotic?
6. Which word on the poster would make you think it was posted on walls some time after the war started and not at the beginning of the war? Why would more men have been needed then?
7. How would an appeal for more men be announced today?

Poster C: Working conditions

RULES

To be observed in these Works and subject to which all persons employed are engaged.

1. Ordinary working hours from 6.20 till 8.20 o'clock; from 9 till 1 o'clock; and from 2 till 5.30 o'clock. On Saturdays work will cease at 1.30 o'clock, but without interval for dinner. Wages will be paid by the hour; and only the number of hours actually worked will be paid for. Any workman commencing work and absenting himself without leave until the termination of the ordinary working day, will not be entitled to payment for any time he may have worked on the day in question.

2. The first two hours of Overtime, Saturdays included, to be paid for as time and a quarter, and further Overtime to count as time and a half; but no time will be counted as Overtime until the ordinary number of hours for the day has been completed. Sunday work, when absolutely necessary, will be paid for as double ordinary time.

3. Workmen on the night shift to start work at 5.30 p.m., and continue until 6.20 o'clock the next morning; intervals for meals from 9 till 9.25 p m., and 1.35 till 2 o'clock a.m. For the hours worked on the night shift, time and a quarter will be paid.

4. Wages will be paid fortnightly on each alternate Saturday, at 1.30 o'clock—to be counted up to the previous Thursday night, and from it the amount of any fines, debts, or damages will be deducted. Men off work on the pay day will not be paid until after those working have received their wages.

5. All hands will enter the Works through the Time Offices at starting time, and also on resuming work after breakfast and dinner. Each workman to draw his Time Board on commencing work; and on resuming work after breakfast and dinner, must, as he enters the Works, take his Token off the Board and put it into the receiving slot. On leaving work each workman to pass out through the Time Offices and hand in his Time Board, with the amount of time worked and for what purpose written thereon, and on each Thursday evening the total amount of the previous week's time to be written thereon. Any breach of this Rule will subject him to a fine, and any workman not delivering his Token or Time Board personally at the times mentioned will forfeit all claim to wages for that day. All workmen passing through the gates during working hours must show their Time Boards to the Gatekeeper and give any explanation that may be demanded as to their business; non-compliance with this will forfeit wages for the day and subject the offender to fine or dismissal.

6. Those provided with Tool Boxes or Lockers to leave the keys thereof at the Office or Store before quitting work, if so ordered.

7. Any one causing disturbance in the Works, neglecting the orders of his Foreman, avoidably absent for more than one day without the leave of his Foreman, bringing spirituous liquors into the Works, or appearing here in a state of intoxication, will be subject to fine or dismissal.

8. Any one carelessly or maliciously breaking, injuring, or defacing any Machine or Tool, altering any Template, removing Shores without leave, or committing any other mischief, to pay the cost of repairing the same, or, in the option of the Employers, to be fined.

9. Those provided with Tools must satisfactorily account for the same before leaving the employment, or the value of any that may be missing will be deducted from the wages due.

10. Any one entering or leaving the Works except by the appointed gates, or carrying out material to ships without having it charged by the Storekeeper and also giving account of same to the Gateman, will be subject to fine or dismissal.

11. No person is allowed to take strangers into any portion of the Works without first having obtained an authorized pass.

12. Any one stopping work, or preparing to stop work before the appointed time, will be fined or dismissed.

13. Any one wasting, injuring, or destroying Oil, Pitch, Tar, Oakum, Paint, Candles, Nails, or any other material, to pay the cost thereof.

14. Any one smoking, or preparing food during working hours, or smoking at any other time near combustile material, will be fined or dismissed.

15. Any one leaving a candle, lamp, or fire burning after use, will be fined.

16. In the event of work being spoiled by the carelessness of workmen, the labour expended thereon will not be paid for, and those in fault will be held responsible for the loss of the material.

We reserve to ourselves the right of fining for any irregularity or offence not specially mentioned in the foregoing Rules.

Shipbuilding and Engineering Works,
Belfast, 30th May, 1888.

HARLAND & WOLFF.

QUESTIONS

1. Work out from the details in no. 1 on this poster
   (a) how many hours people worked each day in Harland & Wolff?
   (b) how many hours they worked each week?
2. Why would they have got time off from 8.20 am to 9 am?
3. How long was the night shift (see no. 3)? What does it mean when it says 'for the hours worked on night shift time and a quarter will be paid'?
4. For what reason might workers lose a day's pay?
5. For what reason could workers be fined or dismissed?
6. How was a careful record kept of the hours worked by each worker?
7. This was an 'agreement worked out between management and the workers' trade union'. What might we consider surprising about this today?

DIARIES AND MEMOIRS

A diary is a personal account of the day-to-day experiences in the life of the writer. Entries in a diary are dated and are usually written at the time of, or shortly after, the events they describe. The great value of diaries is that they sometimes allow us to see how individuals felt about events which were happening at that time.

Memoirs are very like diaries. The main difference is that memoirs are written a considerable time after the events they describe. It is most common for people to write their memoirs after they retire. Memoirs look back at events and may not reveal the immediate feelings of the time in the way a diary would. The writer has had time to think about events and knows what has happened since. This can be an advantage but it can also be a disadvantage if the writer's memory of events is influenced by what has happened afterwards.

Most diaries are meant to be confidential, that is, to be read only by the writer. Personal diaries which are found to contain items of interest to the public may be published after the writer's death with the permission of their relatives.

The diary of Anne Frank

This was the case, for example, with the diary of Anne Frank, a young Jewish girl. Her family went into hiding before the Second World War to escape Hitler's persecution of the Jews. Anne kept a diary which records what it was like to be in hiding for two years. Her family were eventually discovered and taken to a concentration camp where Anne later died. Her father survived and allowed her diary to be published so that those who read it could learn of their suffering and Anne's quiet courage.

Emma Duffin's diaries

Diaries and memoirs have proved to be very useful in letting us see how people felt and what life was like at times in the past. For example, the notebooks of Emma Duffin help us understand what life was like for a young nurse trying to help the wounded in various hospitals in Egypt and France during the First World War.

Photograph of Emma Duffin VAD.

Here are 3 extracts from Emma's diary. The first two describe some of her experiences as a nurse in Egypt and France during the First World War. The third describes her experiences of helping after the Belfast Blitz during the Second World War.

Example A Christmas 1915

"Christmas day was a very strenuous day for everybody. The captain was very musical and had trained a choir of orderlies and MO's (medical officers) and they went all round the wards singing carols, to the great delight of all the patients . . . We had great difficulty in persuading the men that the beds must be made and the tent tidied even if it was Christmas day, especially as we were to be visited by a General and the Matron in Chief. However we at last got things spick and span, attired each of them in a clean shirt and gave them a rose for their button holes and made them look quite smart. I was quite alarmed about two of them who were heart cases and were in such a state of excitement and laughed so much that I was afraid they would make themselves ill.

I thought of the only other Christmas I had even spent away from home, in Germany. We had visited a hospital there too and sung German carols outside the wards and I wondered if they had done it this year and if they had their Christmas trees as usual. . . . It seemed impossible when we thought of all the dreadful things they had done but they had been very good to me and I felt sorry that we could never meet on friendly terms again.

I thought of the patients I had seen that evening when I went in to help. I had found them singing hymns and it had given me a lump in my throat to see some of them so terribly ill and worn singing 'Abide with me' and 'Onward Christian Soldiers', and 'Peace on Earth Goodwill to Men'. We were all singing it and no doubt the Germans were doing the same and what a farce it would seem to an outsider and what hypocrites we ought to appear and yet I know we weren't all hypocrites and all the Germans weren't, though I felt a good many must be. It was impossible to understand and reconcile. What fools we all were. I gave it up as a bad job and went to sleep.

The day after Christmas seemed rather flat and everybody's tempers were a bit short but none of our patients were any the worse for the festivities which was something to be thankful for."

Example B June 1916

"I had not been on night duty very long when the big push began and the trains came and came and the boats did not come fast enough and we worked all night and came on duty again after breakfast and prayed and looked for the boats, especially the 'Asturias' because she was the biggest.

I was sent on duty on the station platform and if the hospital had not made me realise the war I realised it that night; under the big arc lights in the station lay stretchers four deep, so close one could scarcely get one's feet between, all down both platforms. At the end were the walking cases. They were past walking and the majority had lain down huddled together, their arms in slings and their heads bound up, the mud from the trenches sticking to their clothes and the blood still caked on them. I walked up and down all night feeling I was in a bad dream, giving one a drink, another an extra blanket if I could find one, or attempting the hopeless task of trying to make men with their legs in splints a little more comfortable; feeling the pulses of the men who felt faint, rearranging a bandage that had slipped and watching for haemorrhages. . . . In the middle of the night we heard the whistle of another hospital train and my heart sank. Every ward was full. There was scarcely room for another stretcher on the platform and there was no boat. The train crawled slowly in and turned out to be only walking cases waiting for the boat with their Blighty tickets in their buttonholes. Towards morning a boat came in."

Example C September 1939

Introduction

"During the 1914-18 War I kept a diary and though it was not written from day to day it was written while all the events were fresh in my mind and may someday be of interest.

It is unlikely that in this war I will be able to take an active part but having served as a VAD in a military hospital during the last I had, as we have been asked to do, registered again for nursing service at a First Aid Post but, being 25 years older, would only be able to work for short spells. On this account this diary will probably be less interesting and I may later decide that it is not worth keeping but I will begin by recording some of my impressions before and on the outbreak of war."

Emma wrote this in her diary after describing the horror of working in the make-shift morgue in Belfast's markets area after a blitz, helping distraught relatives to look for the bodies of members of their families.

"I came away drawing deep breaths of fresh air. So this was the result of a Blitz. I had heard of it, pictured it, now seen it. I saw in my mind's eye the grey green faces of children, one in a coffin with its mother and the bare foot of a little child, and I heard the voice of a woman in my ears asking for a child, a little boy in "velvet trousers". I tried not to think of it and to think of "whatsoever things are good, whatsoever things are lovely, whatsoever things are of good report" . . . birds, flowers, beautiful skies and seas. Hitler could not distort this."

QUESTIONS

Extract A: Why do you think Emma's feelings towards the Germans were so confused?

Extract B: What does her description tell us about the horror of war?

Extract C: Emma wrote that her diary of the Second World War might not be worth keeping. As a young historian, what is your opinion?

QUESTIONS

1.   In what ways are diaries different from other sources you have considered?
2.   How reliable do you think these diaries are as evidence of the past? Explain your answer.
3.   How could you check Emma's account of what happened?

ORAL HISTORY

**What is
Oral History?**

Oral history involves recording memories of older people who can describe what things were like when they were younger. The historian asks them a series of questions and the answers are recorded, usually on tape. A written record of the interview is also made and the original tape recording is kept. These oral records can be used as evidence of the past.

Older people are often interviewed about changes which have occurred in their lifetime, for example, about their days at school; the food they ate; the jobs they were employed to do; their memories of being unemployed; how they spent their leisure time; where they went on holidays, etc. Often the interviews are about their memories of special events of national importance, such as war or great sporting events they attended.

In the past, historians have been reluctant to admit that oral history and the memories of older people are a valuable source for the study of history. They have preferred to use written evidence. One of the first historians to use oral history, Paul Thompson, said that:

"in contrast to any other historical document, oral evidence comes from a living source. If it seems misleading it is possible to ask for more. Documents cannot answer back but oral history is a two-way process. It is not dependent on documents but it can indeed lead to their discovery and living people can offer a historian more than evidence".

These extracts tells us a lot about social life and conditions in the past.

**Extract 1
School**

'When I was at school we had very few books. We learned to write using a slate-pencil on a piece of slate. It used to make a scratchy sound and when twenty or thirty of us were writing, it used to make my flesh creep. I can tell you I was very glad when we began to use jotters and lead-pencils. Next we were taught to write with pen and ink and I had a terrible time because I was left-handed. You weren't allowed to be left-handed so I had to try to write with the right. As soon as the master's back was turned I used the left, so to put a stop to this he used to tie my left hand behind my back with my neck-tie. He would hardly get away with that nowadays.'

'It was very cold in school except for the rooms which had coal fires. The teacher's desk sat on a little platform so that he or she could see everything that was going on. The teacher would have caned you if you so much as talked — on the knuckles and on the backs of the legs. You had no materials for counting or for helping you to learn fractions or tables. You just had to learn them off by heart from the black-board. You had to learn your spellings and tables perfectly otherwise you got the cane.'

'The master wouldn't put up with any talk at all. He had a big cane and if you hadn't your homework done you got the cane.'

'There were two classrooms — really they were one large hall with wooden doors in the middle. Fireplaces sat at either end and each morning the children had to bring a penny or some coal for the fire. If they failed to bring either they were not allowed to stand anywhere near the fire and so they were frozen. On very cold days the doors in the centre were opened and the pupils marched round the hall singing to keep warm.'

'Some children used to come to school in their bare feet even in the dead of winter.'

Extract 2
Sickness

Before the days of the NHS medical attention was costly:
'The fear of the doctor's bill made people turn to home-remedies and folkcures or to the person who had the cure. It wasn't only the country people who believed in folk-medicine; I knew plenty of ones in Belfast who used it all the time.'

'I always suffered from sore throats. My mother would make a tube out of paper and use it to blow sulphur down my throat. As well as that she would fill a sock with salt and heat it and placed it round my neck. It always worked.'

'When I was young Tuberculosis (or TB as it was called) was a killer disease. Several of my schoolmates died from it. Young people who caught it had to be kept separate from the rest of the family; usually in a wooden shed in the back-yard. The mass X-Ray and better housing in the post-war period helped to make the disease a thing of the past.'

Extract 3
Entertainment

People provided their own entertainment in bygone days:
'Around the fire on winter nights we sang songs and played music on the paper and comb. Sometimes we would have a bowl of soapy water and a clay pipe and then we would blow bubbles.'

'On Sunday nights we gathered round the piano and my mother would play hymns and we all joined in. We had no gramophone, no wireless, and, of course no television — it had not been invented yet.'

'Our evenings were spent listening to the neighbours who used to call to *ceilidhe* in our house. They told all sorts of stories and talked about what was going on in the townland. Fairs and markets were discussed as well as the price of cattle. We had great times in the long winter nights.'

'Very often in a night's *ceilidhing* in the country numerous ghost stories would be told and, by the time it came to bedtime, the children of the house would have been so frightened that they could hardly have faced going up their own stairs. With only a single spluttering candle to light the way, they became aware of menacing shadows lurking in every corner. Every shadow and shape took on a sinister appearance. Even a small thorn bush outside the back door suddenly became the silhouette of a bogey-man waiting to pounce on anyone who passed. Many an adult would have been afraid to go home alone especially if his path led past an old graveyard and some of the neighbours might have to convey him along the loneliest stretch of the road.'

'Hallow Eve is nothing now like what it used to be. We had great fun ducking for apples in a basin of water. You nearly got drowned. When all the apples were finished, we dressed up in old clothes and blackened our faces with soot and went round the doors asking 'Anything for Hallow Eve?' Bigger fellows (I suppose you would call them 'teenagers' nowadays) would play tricks on people, taking off gates, or tying a thread to a door-knocker and knocking the door from a safe distance.'

QUESTIONS

1. *Extract 1*
    What extra information does this source give us about schools which we could not get from school registers?
2. *Extract 2*
    Why is oral history particularly important in preserving this type of information?
3. *Extract 3*
    Why was story-telling such an important form of entertainment in the past?
4. What are the advantages of using oral history as a source?
5. What may be the disadvantages of using oral history as evidence?
6. How can an historian overcome some of the disadvantages of oral history?

CASE STUDY

ULSTER DAY: THE SIGNING OF ULSTER'S SOLEMN LEAGUE AND COVENANT

As we have seen, different types of evidence can help us to understand the history of our country. This evidence can take a variety of forms — from the remains of food people ate in the Early Christian period (Archaeological Evidence), to reports to the government during the Famine (Parliamentary Papers), to the personal recollections of a nurse in the First and Second World Wars (Diaries).

But how reliable are the sources which we use to build a picture of the past? Historians, for example, sometimes differ in the way in which they interpret the evidence. When looking at sources it is extremely important to keep an open mind, to weigh up all the evidence and to reach balanced conclusions based on all viewpoints. Let us try to do this by examining a relatively recent event in Ulster's history — the signing of the Solemn League and Covenant in 1912. In this case study it is possible to see how different evidence presents many different views of this event. Historians must examine this evidence and explain not only what happened but also try to explain why it occurred and how it should be interpreted.

The background to Ulster Day

In the late nineteenth and early part of the twentieth century, keeping or breaking Ireland's political Union with Britain was the most important issue in Irish politics. Keeping the Union was mostly supported by Protestants (Unionists) who made up about 25% of the population of Ireland. Most of these Protestants lived in the north-eastern part of the country where they out-numbered the Roman Catholics. Their leader was Sir Edward Carson. Ending the Union was mostly supported by Roman Catholics (Nationalists) who wanted either to break it completely or replace it with 'home rule'. Home rule would have given Ireland her own parliament, probably in Dublin.

When Home Rule Bills were proposed by the British government in 1886 and 1893 the Unionists protested and there was rioting in Belfast. The Bills were defeated. In 1912, the British government was again considering the possibility of introducing home rule to Ireland. The Unionists were now better organised than they had been and they decided to show their opposition.

Ulster Day

A 'day of declaration' was organised for 28 September 1912. This day was to be the climax of a whole week of events, demonstrations and meetings against home rule throughout the province of Ulster. The 28 September, or Ulster Day, was to be regarded as a public holiday. Union Jacks were flown in the streets, free Bibles were distributed, 'Orange' arches were erected and special religious services were held. The most important part of the day was the signing of the Solemn League and Covenant which declared:

Being convinced in our consciences that Home Rule would be disastrous to the material well-being of Ulster as well as the whole of Ireland, subversive of our civil and religious freedom, destructive of our citizenship and perilous to the unity of the Empire, we, whose names are underwritten, men of Ulster, loyal subjects of His Gracious Majesty King George V, humbly relying on the God whom our fathers in days of stress and trial confidently trusted, do hereby pledge ourselves in solemn Covenant throughout this our time of threatened calamity to stand by one another in defending for ourselves and our children our cherished position of equal citizenship in the United Kingdom and in using all means which may be found necessary to defeat the present conspiracy to set up a Home Rule Parliament in Ireland. And in the event of such a Parliament being forced upon us we further solemnly and mutually pledge ourselves to refuse to recognize its authority. In sure confidence that God will defend the right we hereto subscribe our names. And further, we individually declare that we have not already signed this Covenant.

An estimated 218,000 men signed the Covenant and a supporting declaration was also signed by about the same number of women. (Women did not have the right to vote in 1912 so female signatures may not have been considered as important as male signatures.) Supporters of Unionism in Britain could also sign a similar document. Each signatory gave their name and address. Some felt so strongly that they also provided a personal opinion. Folk memory also relates that some people signed the Covenant with their own blood.

The signing of the Covenant shows the strength and determination of opposition to home rule in Ulster. Compare the different types of evidence below and see what conclusions can be drawn about Ulster Day 1912.

Contemporary Accounts

DOCUMENT A

Ulster's

Solemn League and Covenant.

Being convinced in our consciences that Home Rule would be disastrous to the material well-being of Ulster as well as of the whole of Ireland, subversive of our civil and religious freedom, destructive of our citizenship and perilous to the unity of the Empire, we, whose names are underwritten, men of Ulster, loyal subjects of His Gracious Majesty King George V., humbly relying on the God whom our fathers in days of stress and trial confidently trusted, do hereby pledge ourselves in solemn Covenant throughout this our time of threatened calamity to stand by one another in defending for ourselves and our children our cherished position of equal citizenship in the United Kingdom and in using all means which may be found necessary to defeat the present conspiracy to set up a Home Rule Parliament in Ireland. ¶ And in the event of such a Parliament being forced upon us we further solemnly and mutually pledge ourselves to refuse to recognise its authority. ¶ In sure confidence that God will defend the right we hereto subscribe our names. ¶ And further, we individually declare that we have not already signed this Covenant.

The above was signed by me at ....
"Ulster Day," Saturday, 28th September, 1912.

Edward Carson

——— God Save the King. ———

DOCUMENT B

Irish News, (a Belfast nationalist newspaper)

The farce was played out to the very last 'scene' of the elaborately staged production. . . . A 'covenant' had been signed by a great number of people, many of whom had never read its terms — nor will they ever read the document. . . . From start to finish the demonstration of 'play-acting' was designed to impress the people of Great Britain and . . . to intimidate Protestant Home Rulers in the north of Ireland.

At last the curtain has been hung down on the Ulster Day farce, and we may hope for, at any rate, a temporary return to that civic sanity of which Belfast prides itself so tremendously. The Carsonite circus . . . gave its final and greatest performance, entitled 'Signing the Covenant' in Belfast on Saturday and wound up its fantastic career in a paroxysm of flag-waving and noise emblematic of the meaningless nonsense of the whole grotesque scheme from start to finish.

DOCUMENT C

Belfast News Letter, (a unionist newspaper)

Ulster Day, so eagerly anticipated and prepared for with such care and organizing skill, has come and gone, leaving behind it memories that will make the 28 September 1912 a date never to be forgotten in the annals of the Imperial province. The proceedings of the day were characterized by an enthusiasm and, at the same time, a solemnity which heightened their impressiveness, and nothing was wanting to emphasise the importance and significance of the occasion.

Never in the history of Belfast was the city more gaily decorated than on Saturday last. . . . The suburbs, in common with the centre of the city, were ablaze with colour, and the predominating feature was the innumerable Union Jacks — symbolic of the unity of the Empire — which fluttered proudly in the breeze from the leading commercial and industrial establishments, from the stately mansions of the rich, and from the humble homes of the poor.

DOCUMENT D

The Observer, (a London Sunday newspaper)

Through the mass, with drums and fifes, sashes and banners, the clubs marched all day. The streets surged with cheering, but still no disorder, still no policemen, still no shouts of rage or insult. Yet no-one for a moment could have mistaken the concentrated will and courage of these people. They do not know what fear and flinching mean in this business, and they are not going to know. They do not, indeed, believe it possible that they can be beaten, but no extremity, the worst, will ever see them ashamed.

DOCUMENT E

Photograph: Women signing the Covenant declaration in Belfast, 28 September 1912.

DOCUMENT F

Photograph: A religious service outside the City Hall, Belfast, before the signing of the Covenant.

DOCUMENT G

> 'The Covenanters
> Stand still, old earth! Circle no more sun
> Today, in truth, a fateful thing is done.
> In Ulster's North-East corner, where they breed
> Vile hatred of a 'Papist' for his creed.
>
> And thus upon this day they have decreed
> Their 'covenant' of privilege and greed
> And shattered with a stroke, the hollow thing
> They called their 'Loyalty to Throne and King!'

(J F quoted in 'The Irish News')

DOCUMENT H

Contemporary commemoration of Ulster Day

> 'Who shall dare to sever
> Ulster from the Union?
> Ulster's Sons shall ever
> Smit them hip and thigh
> Or rejoice to die
> In the grand endeavour . . .'

Interpretations of Ulster Day by Historians

DOCUMENT I

F. S. L. Lyons

'The Unionists in general, and Carson in particular, devoted themselves to raising the tension in Ulster to a raw high pitch. . . . What gave this tribal ritual its real menace was the fact that Ulstermen were beginning to drill and to organise in support of their threats'.

DOCUMENT J

A. T. Q. Stewart

'This was their will. A democratic deed had been done. A people knew its mind and had signed and sealed a Covenant of its inflexible resolve'.

DOCUMENT K

D. W. Harkness

'It was, after all, a propaganda rallying cry, a call to action in the face of a worst possible scenario forecast. We can admire it as such, but we do not have to accept its assertions. We can recognise its effectiveness and the genuine fears lying behind it, but we must still see it for what it was and what it tells us about those who wrote it and who signed it'.

DOCUMENT L

P. Buckland

'The signing of the covenant was an impressive demonstration of Ulster unionist discipline and determination. . . . Yet something more than demonstrations was required. . . . On the one hand, nationalists and liberals continued to doubt Ulster unionist sincerity . . . on the other hand, the longer the crisis was prolonged the greater was the danger of the rank and file would take matters into their own hands. By 1913 the Ulster unionist leaders were under increasing pressure to take provocative action of one form or another'.

QUESTIONS

1   Consult Documents A and F
   (a)   Why, according to the Solemn League and Covenant, did Ulster Unionists oppose home rule?
   (b)   Why do you think that Ulster Unionists found it necessary to describe as a 'conspiracy' the attempt to set up a home rule parliament in Ireland?
   (c)   On the evidence contained within these documents, how far do you think that Ulster Unionists believed that they had God on their side?

2.   Consult Document B
   (a)   On what grounds does the *Irish News* describe the events of Ulster Day as mere 'play-acting' and 'meaningless nonsense'?
   (b)   Why do you think that the *Irish News* is trying to discredit Ulster Day?

3.   Consult Documents C, E and F
   (a)   Do you attach any significance to the fact that the women signing the Covenant in Document E are all well-dressed?
   (b)   How far, if at all, do these documents contradict the view that Covenant Day was 'play-acting' and 'meaningless nonsense'?

4.   Consult Document D
   What impression do you think that people in Great Britain might have gained of Covenant Day?

5.   Consult Documents B, C, G and H
   Which do you think are more effective in conveying feelings about, and the atmosphere of, Covenant Day — the verses (G and H), or the prose (B and C)?

6.   Consult Documents I, J, K and L
   The historians each emphasise different aspects of Ulster Day.
   (a)   On the basis of the evidence contained in Documents A-H, which interpretation do you prefer, giving reasons why you prefer that interpretation?
   (b)   Why do you think that historians adopt different views of issues and events, such as Ulster Day?

7.   Do any members of your family have stories to tell you about Ulster Day, 1912? If so, what do their stories add to the impression of Ulster Day you have gained from Documents A-L?